Praise for FREEZE-FRAME

"The intensity of our present world sometimes makes it difficult to stay in balance. Efficient techniques for inner self-management are an absolute must for the personal survival list of present and future humanity. *FREEZE-FRAME* is an excellent guide to the why's and how's. It is phrased in a beautifully simple way that I enjoyed immensely."

WILLIAM A. TILLER, Ph.D., Professor Emeritus, Dept. of Materials Science and Engineering, Stanford University

"FREEZE-FRAME and the techniques taught by the Institute of HeartMath are the cutting edge. Their practice bestows confidence that you can manage any situation, whether personal or professional."

ALAN WATKINS, M.D., Research Fellow, Dept. of Medicine, Southampton University, England

"FREEZE-FRAME works as advertised — a one minute power tool that transforms stressful reactions into productive and efficient actions. FREEZE-FRAME helps create a quality culture of care and . . . gives us freedom to focus on the task at hand without being distracted by negative thought loops, unsatisfactory communication, emotional baggage, and feelings of insecurity or anxiety about the future."

MAJOR RICK T. REESE, Chief, Wing Quality, Falcon Air Force Base

"Surprisingly simple!"

INCENTIVE MAGAZINE

"A proven technique to reduce anxiety and health care costs."

WORKSITE WELLNESS WORKS

D0951844

"*FREEZE-FRAME* is not just about a technique, it is about a way of approaching every stressful part of your life. The heart of the message (pun intended) is the very FREEZE-FRAME act itself and how the reader can use it to bring a more centered, grounded, and stress-free approach to professional and personal situations."

JAMES A. AUTRY, author, *Love and Profit: The Art of Caring Leadership*, and *Life and Work: A Manager's Search for Meaning*

"Freeze-framing helps us to be proactive and spend more time in creating an environment that facilitates planning and collaboration rather than crisis and demands."

JUDY ARMSTRONG, Group Director, Management Information Systems, Cadence Design Systems

"I've been working with the quality programs in the Air Force and we had a lot of frustration in meetings, taking an hour and a half or more on very simple projects. I began to FREEZE-FRAME right before meetings for two reasons: to make sure I was prepared, and to get myself into a frame of mind so I could listen better in the meetings to provide better facilitation. The last meeting was completed in 35 minutes. FREEZE-FRAME has been very productive for me."

MAJOR MICHAEL MORSE, United States Air Force

"Amazing results! A real energy saver."

SUN REPORTER

"The FREEZE-FRAME technique is an excellent way to increase your leverage in any sport without sacrificing your fun or your health."

HAWAII TENNIS NEWS

"*FREEZE-FRAME* should be required reading in managerial training programs to increase work performance and obtain a greater sense of fulfillment. High-level government employees can often lose touch with the moment and become engulfed in the process of what is happening around them. FREEZE-FRAME is an effective means to re-evaluate the situation and provide an appropriate, understanding, and caring response."

JIM L'ETOILE, Assistant Director, Office of Substance Abuse Programs, Department of Corrections, State of California

"The tool is ingenious in its simplicity, easily accessible and user friendly. [The benefits include] increased productivity and concentration, increased appreciation for colleagues/family, decreased gossipy mindsets, heightened creativity and intuition."

PAUL GIROUX, Senior Consultant, Mainstream Access Corp.

"It's amazing how a 15-second FREEZE-FRAME can change everything."

J.S., age 14

"[FREEZE-FRAME] is clearly on the cutting edge in the hugely popular field of self-improvement."

LINCOLN (NE) JOURNAL

"If you find yourself feeling overwhelmed by life, read *FREEZE-FRAME*. This one-minute technique can help you reduce stress, lessen emotional pain and improve the clarity of your decision-making. The power to eliminate the effects of stress in our lives is within us, we have only to learn how to use it."

SCOOP USA

DEDICATION

*This book is dedicated to those in need of quick stress release —
something that works now.*

By DOC LEW CHILDRE

*Self Empowerment: The Heart Approach to
Stress Management*
The How To Book of Teen Self Discovery
Heart Zones (cassette and CD)
Speed of Balance (cassette and CD)

FREEZE-FRAME®

Fast Action Stress Relief

A Scientifically Proven Technique

by

Doc Lew Childre

Edited by Bruce Cryer

PLANETARY PUBLICATIONS

Boulder Creek, California

Copyright © 1994 Planetary Publications

All rights reserved. No part of this book may be reproduced or trans-mitted in any form or by any means, electronic or mechanical, in-cluding photocopying, recording, or by any information storage and retrieval system without permission in writing from the publisher.

FREEZE-FRAME is a registered trademark of the Institute of HeartMath.

Published in the United States of America by:

Planetary Publications

P.O. Box 66, Boulder Creek, California 95006

(800) 372-3100   (408) 338-2161   Fax (408) 338-9861

Manufactured in the United States of America by R.R. Donnelley & Sons Co.

First Printing 1994
Second Printing 1995

Cover Design by Sandy Royall

Library of Congress Cataloging in Publication Data

Childre, Doc Lew,   1945-
      Freeze-frame : a scientifically proven technique ... / by Doc Lew Childre
      p. cm.
      Includes bibliographical references.
      ISBN 1-879052-39-3 : $9.95
          1. Stress management.   I. Title
RA785.C448   1994
616.9'8--dc20   94-13447
                                                                CIP

10 9 8 7 6 5 4 3 2

Table of Contents

Why People Need a Tool Like FREEZE-FRAME

The pressure's building. You feel *so* steamed up that your gauge has hit the danger zone and your lid is about to blow. It's been one thing after another and you just can't take it anymore. You have to get away, take a walk on the beach, a hike in the mountains, or a drive in the country. Once you get there, you begin to cool down and let a little steam out. At this point you experience a change in perspective. Some creative solutions that had escaped you while under pressure now become clear. Wouldn't it be *great* if you could have that same clarity and insight *in the moment when stress is happening*? You can, and this book will show you how.

The world has become a pressure cooker, with the burden of stress growing daily. It's hard to ignore stress in the '90s, especially with the media constantly reminding us just how bad life is — youth violence, ethnic violence, drugs, unemployment, the homeless, floods, earthquakes, a decaying educational system in the U.S., and the challenge of globalization. Our mind and emotions are bombarded daily with information that reinforces just how stressed we *should* feel. Experts say stress has become an epidemic: 75 to 90% of all doctor visits in the U.S. today are for stress-related disorders. Even the statistics can be stressful:

♦ Disabling stress has doubled over the last six years.

♦ Seventy-two percent of American workers experience frequent, stress-related physical or mental conditions that greatly increase health care costs.

♦ Forty percent of employee turnover is due to stress.

♦ One million employees per day are absent from work due to stress-related disorders.

Science has shown us that we pay a serious price for our stress. Eighty percent of all disease is now believed to be stress-related. A 20-year study conducted by the University of London School of Medicine has determined that unmanaged mental and emotional reactions to stress present a more dangerous risk factor for cancer and heart disease than cigarette smoking or eating high cholesterol foods.

So, with a growing list of things to feel stressed about, what do we do? Fold up our tents and go home? Give our boss notice and not go back to work? Sell the car so we don't have to deal with rush hour traffic anymore?

The central message of this book is: *There is hope*

because there is a solution. Recent scientific research has proven that we can learn not only to manage our stress, but even to prevent much of it before it happens. The key is within our hearts. As we learn to *prevent* stress, we save a tremendous amount of energy — energy that can be used to develop creative projects, build fulfilling relationships, solve family problems, make more effective decisions, and have more fun. It's simple.

Does that mean that if we learn this technique called FREEZE-FRAME, the boss will stop being so demanding, or the company will reverse its decision to lay off 10% of the work force, or our kids will suddenly turn into the little angels we wish they would be? No, but it does mean that no matter what life throws our way, we will have more strength, flexibility, and common sense to deal with it. This book was written to offer people a chance to try the first step in the HeartMath system of personal energy management and empowerment. HeartMath teaches people how to listen to their hearts to awaken more of their own intuitive intelligence. The FREEZE-FRAME technique is simple, but don't let its simplicity fool you. Try it out.

In this book you will learn how much you can prosper and profit as you learn to FREEZE-FRAME. How using this technique can help you be more productive at work. How it can improve the health of your heart and immune system, and even slow the aging process. How it can give your mind more clarity. How it can help your emotions bring you more fun and adventure. How it can bring more quality to your relationships. And, how you can take back control of your life. No one likes to feel victimized — by people, issues or especially, yourself. There's no need to, anymore.

Chapter One

A Typical Stressful Day

It's been a typical day at the office for Nick: Too many interruptions. A staff meeting that went longer than planned. An additional two-week delay on a key shipment. He is already running late to pick up his daughter Tracy from high school, and the day's events are spinning in his mind. It hasn't been a terrible day really, just the usual stress and strain. As Nick pulls onto the freeway, there are more red taillights staring at him than usual. "Damn! I'm going to be really late for Tracy."

Nick sees the right lane closed up ahead for repaving. His mind and emotions race with frustration, triggering a sequence of physical changes inside his body, unbeknownst to him. His emotional reaction is causing large amounts of adrenaline and the stress hormone cortisol to enter his bloodstream. The stress response is in full gear. As the adrenaline reaches Nick's heart, his heart begins to pound harder and harder. A little voice tells him to relax — "the traffic can't move until it moves" —

but he ignores it and his frustration mounts into resentment.

The excess adrenaline and cortisol are causing his immune system to shut down — not a good idea when you're under stress. The portion of his nervous system that normally would have calmed his heart is also shut down, so his heart keeps pumping out blood as though it were a life and death situation — more than he would ever need just sitting there in traffic. There are other effects too: sweaty palms, rapid breathing. All these physical responses send messages back to the brain reinforcing the perception of danger — drowning out the little voice telling him to relax.

By now Nick is knee-deep in feeling victimized: "What a lousy day! When are they going to widen this freeway? Why can't my wife pick up Tracy?" The adrenaline, still going strong, causes yet another hidden effect in Nick. It is stimulating the release of fat cells into his bloodstream — he would have needed this extra energy if it had been a real emergency. Only it isn't. So, unbeknownst to him, his liver is converting the fat into cholesterol which is absorbed onto a scratch that just formed on his coronary artery. Some even gets stuck on the artery wall itself.*

Just then, the traffic starts to move and Nick heaves a huge sigh of relief. But the damage has been done. Drained and irritated, he jams down hard on the accelerator to race to his daughter's school, narrowly missing the side of an 18-wheeler whose driver quickly lets Nick

* Editor's note: Some of the physiological information in this chapter is based on the work of Dr. Redford Williams, chairman of the Dept. of Behavioral Science at Duke University. His book, *Anger Kills* (Times Books) explains the stress response in detail.

know how he feels about his driving. Nick finally pulls up to the school where an impatient Tracy is in a phone booth calling to find out where Dad is. During the ride home, she asks to borrow the car for a party, and Nick blows up at her. A stony silence develops between them, and when they reach the house, Tracy races to her room in tears, "Why does Dad treat me like a child?" Nick then unloads on his wife Maria what a crummy day it has been. Without waiting for her to respond, he flops into the armchair and turns on the TV.

This all too common scenario gets replayed daily, with variations, all over the world. While some of the events in Nick's day are beyond his control, his responses could be much different — if he knew how to manage his emotional reactions to these events.

Stress and the Heart

When the father-daughter war bursts into the house, Maria is busy reading some articles her manager gave her on stress and a new technique called FREEZE-FRAME. "Boy, Nick and Tracy could use this!" she thinks. Instead of jumping up to try to calm the ruffled feathers, she decides to stay put and keep on reading.

The statistics on stress seem alarming at first, though she has to admit they are quite believable. Excerpts from a book called *The Language of the Heart*, by James Lynch, Ph.D., lay out the effects on the heart.

- ♦ For the past three to four decades, cardiovascular disease has led the list of killers in virtually every industrialized society.

- ♦ Heart disease now accounts for slightly more

than 50% of all deaths reported in the United States.

♦ Hypertension, or sustained elevated blood pressure, has long been recognized as a leading contributor to a variety of cardiovascular diseases, including stroke and heart attacks. Hypertensive individuals are two to three times more likely to develop coronary artery disease than those with normal blood pressure, and are four times more likely to suffer a stroke.

♦ It has been estimated that approximately sixty million Americans are hypertensive. High blood pressure may damage the lining of blood vessels which supply blood to vital organs such as the brain, heart, kidneys, and eyes, resulting in the clinical manifestations of hypertension, such as stroke, heart attack, heart and kidney failure. Since hypertension usually presents no detectable symptoms until secondary-organ damage occurs, medical scientists have labeled this disease "America's number-one silent killer."

"Hypertension?" Even the *word* sounds stressful! "I wonder if Nick's short fuse means he has hypertension? And what about Tracy? Her grades have been falling and she hasn't seemed happy lately. Can FREEZE-FRAME help her, too?" (Yes, it can, as you'll read later.)

As Maria thumbs through the materials, she finds an article in the *Wall Street Journal* with statistics on stress in children that add to her concerns.

♦ "I estimate that as many as 35% of the nation's

children have moderate to extreme stress."
Michael Bernard, New York Institute for Rational-Emotive Therapy

♦ "Children are more stressed than ever and stress is expected to mount as youngsters are pushed to tackle academic and other responsibilities for which they aren't developmentally prepared."
Phillip Kendall, Director, Temple University Child and Adolescent Anxiety Disorders Clinic

♦ "Outside of certain school programs, no one is communicating to children how to deal with stressful situations."
Donna Wolf, Stress Consultant

Now Maria really wants to know what FREEZE-FRAME is and how it can help her family.

Stress and Personal Power

What Maria reads intrigues her. FREEZE-FRAME is designed to help release stress — even if you have a poor diet, are overweight, or lack regular exercise. It does this by helping you balance your system from the inside-out and increase personal power. Essi Systems, a San Francisco-based stress-research consulting firm, has discovered important new data on the relationship between personal power and stress. Their research explains why most stress reduction programs don't work. They have found that what's usually taught — diet, physical fitness, not smoking and weight control — have a negligible effect on a person's ability to cope with work pressures or rapid change. According to Essi's findings, the only factor with any significant impact on a person's ability to withstand work pressure is "personal power" — having control over your time, resources, important information, work load and so on. Essi's founder, Esther Orioli, states, "Our testing revealed that out of 21 stress-related factors we examined, personal power was the only factor that could predict who got sick and who stayed healthy in work situations with high amounts of pressure. Conversely, people without this sense of personal power tended to feel victimized and were unable to cope with high amounts of pressure in similar situations."

"Of course!" Maria responds. Nick has felt totally overwhelmed since the company went through its restructuring. He has more responsibility, more hours, less fun, less feeling of control over his future. And she remembers how it feels when she has to deal with rapid change herself. She gets tired easily and her stress level is definitely higher.

The Stress Response

Researchers have analyzed the stress response in microscopic detail. They have discovered that perpetual releases of the hormones adrenaline, noradrenaline and cortisol sear the body like a drizzle of acid. They also believe that, if left unchecked, chronic stress, along with attitudes like hostility, anger and depression, can sicken and eventually kill us.

Dr. Robert Sapolsky, a MacArthur Fellow and Stanford University biologist, has studied stress for 12 years. He recently found strong evidence that chronic stress causes significant brain damage in rats. His work suggests "the total amount of one class of stress hormone you're exposed to determines how much brain damage you get in aging. [In rats and apparently in monkeys] senility is caused by stress." Dr. Sapolsky is not the only researcher who has seen the link between stress and aging of brain cells. Studies indicate possible stress-related factors in Alzheimer's disease and other age-related disorders.

Research at the Institute of HeartMath indicates that *the amount of stress we feel is based on our perception of a person, place, or event, far more than the event itself.* For example, after the 1989 Loma Prieta earthquake near San Francisco, interviews with survivors revealed a wide range of reactions that were unrelated to the severity of their losses. Many people moved away from the state, determined to never again go through such a terrifying experience. Others needed therapy to speed the healing from their trauma. However, there were those who lost their homes yet adapted quickly and expressed appreciation that the community had truly come together as a family, neighbors helping neighbors, the way life is supposed to be. For everyone in the San Francisco Bay Area, the 7.1 earthquake was a very stressful event. But people's ability to bounce back, pick up the pieces and move on with their lives was directly related to their *perceptions* of what had occurred. Those who recovered their lives most quickly and successfully did not remain victims. They realized, like it or not, since they couldn't change what had happened, it made common sense to adapt and move on with life as quickly as possible.

Maria begins to realize that *learning how to FREEZE-FRAME means understanding how to choose your perceptions so they are the most healthful and productive possible.* This builds personal power.

By now, the pieces of the puzzle are starting to fall into place for her. All the scientific research makes perfect sense. She can recall times in their marriage when she and Nick have had a major argument, and then, within a day or two, one of them has gotten a cold or other illness. She knows it is often much easier to help someone else with their frustration and anxiety than to help herself. Maria wished she could have that same clear perspective when she is in the middle of *her own stress and strain*! She realizes there are many times she doesn't stop to listen to her deeper self even when it's giving her solutions to her own stress. In fact, she often kicks herself for not listening to her instincts. Now she realizes she could save a lot of energy, hassle, and tired and worn out feelings with — FREEZE-FRAME!

Chapter Two

The Purpose of FREEZE-FRAME

Why do I call it "FREEZE-FRAME?" When you watch a movie, what you are seeing is a series of still frames on film that are moving rapidly. Life can often seem like a high speed movie that keeps getting faster without our knowing how to slow it down. How you *choose* to respond each moment to the movie of life determines how you see the next frame, and the next, and eventually how you feel when the movie ends. When you're mentally or emotionally reacting to life — with frustration, anxiety, indecision, etc. — you are releasing self-poisoning stress hormones into your system, draining your energy and distorting your perspective. Consequently, your next choice may not be an intelligent one. FREEZE-FRAME enhances the power to stop your reaction to the movie at any moment, call "time-out" and get a clearer perspective on how to adapt to what's happening on the screen. Instead of *self-poisoning*, you gain *self-poise*. Anyone can do it.

In the past you have been told, "Stop and count to ten" or "Think positive." Or nowadays you might hear "Chill out." If you try counting to ten, frequently by "three" your emotions feel like a bottle of shaken up club soda ready to pop! Often people go to a quiet place, take a walk on the beach or go jogging when they need clarity. FREEZE-FRAME can work quickly right where you are. It's like bringing that walk on the beach right back to you in a moment — when you're rushing to meet a deadline or in a tense staff meeting or in an argument and can't get away to unwind. You need something to give you more clarity **right now**! That's what FREEZE-FRAME is for.

Have you ever been obsessed with worry or indecision, and finally told yourself "I'm not going to think about it anymore!?" Generally that's easier said than done. The same thoughts keep turning up. With Freeze-Framing you can neutralize those thoughts, allow yourself to find a clearer perspective and handle the situation efficiently and effectively with less energy drain.

Have you also noticed how swiftly life's events can change your moods? You could be walking down the street, feeling angry at something. Suddenly the laughter and joy of a baby seizes your attention. You smile; life's okay again even if you were in a bad mood a 'frame' before. Passing a favorite store, you spot a half-price sale going on. It's the store that has the leather jackets you like so much and the one you've wanted is on sale! Your whole mood shifts. Hormonally, you've changed too — you experience an obvious uplift as you make your purchase and leave. Then, as you walk into an electronics store with dozens of TVs on the wall, you're lured by the latest crisis on CNN – LIVE, as it's happening. Your mood crashes once more. FREEZE-FRAME is an opportunity to make on-the-spot attitude adjustments so life doesn't entrap you in an emotional roller coaster.

Kids are often better at letting go than adults. They can be in a knock-down, drag-out fight on the playground one minute, then, as the emotional steam subsides, be best friends again a few minutes later. It usually takes adults much longer, because the developed adult mind wants to replay the angry thoughts and feelings repeatedly. This habit depletes you from inside-out. Practicing FREEZE-FRAME can help you break the distress cycle, preventing emotional wear and tear on your energy system.

It's a natural caring instinct to try to calm children when they are upset or hurt. People will become innovative and remind the children about something fun they're going to do tomorrow, or assure them that the friend who just grabbed their toy really is a good person. This is done to help children calm down and become still so they can listen and get help. Freeze-Framing is a mature look at that stillness we all know children need. We need it too.

Here's a common scenario: Two people are arguing and resenting each other. After they emotionally exhaust themselves, one of them finally realizes — what a waste of time! But they've already drained a lot of energy. Preventing that drain is the intention of this one-minute technique. FREEZE-FRAME doesn't take the spice out of life; it gives you the opportunity to manage yourself so the fun times can be even more fun, and the down times aren't so down.

Taming the Emotional Monster — Becoming Neutral

Thoughts and feelings play a major role in everything we do. It is through these elements that we experience our happiness, peace of mind, or the worst day we've ever had. Freeze-Framing is especially valuable for learning to go to "neutral" when your mind or emotions are churning. By *neutral* I mean backing off from the uncontrolled emotional reactions. (Chapter Four explains how this benefits your health by slowing the aging process, preventing unnecessary strain on the heart, etc.) Life will still be life. You're not going to change every unpleasant situation simply by Freeze-Framing, but you can save yourself from being drained and depleted time after time.

Take the example of traffic. Many people feel victimized by traffic before the work day has even begun. Traffic can get people frustrated, angry, resentful, or just depressingly accepting. But no matter how they react, the traffic still won't move until it moves. FREEZE-FRAME won't free up the traffic lane. It's designed to keep *you* from aging needlessly before the traffic moves.

Traffic is not the only culprit. Many situations in life — particularly involving certain people we know — can provoke anger, judgment or fear. As you practice FREEZE-FRAME, you learn how to remain calm in those situations so you don't make decisions you'll later regret. The technique creates a harmonious relationship between your head and heart feelings so you can acquire clarity and make smart moves in life.

Here's an analogy for how this tool works. When you are learning a skill like golf or tennis or dance, or even a dangerous physical skill like sky-diving, the teacher will instruct you to relax and find a flow and rhythm with it. The teacher is telling you to FREEZE-

FRAME that part of you which is tense, rigid, and producing stress. The great athletes or dancers are those who can relax as they focus on what they're doing. Much higher performance is invariably the result. With the Freeze-Framing technology, you learn to employ that exact principle with any task or mental and emotional activity.

An additional analogy would be an intense game of basketball. When Team A senses they're losing their cool because Team B is "in sync" and running away with the game, Team A calls a time-out. Why? Team A knows:

◆ If they slow things down for a couple of minutes, they can obtain a clearer perspective of what's happening and start functioning better as a team.

◆ They can formulate some quick adjustments to attempt to switch the momentum back to their side.

◆ They can take time-out to recover lost energy and recharge.

◆ They can regain their composure after feeling "victimized" by how well Team B was playing. The coach can encourage them to "go for it" and put more heart into their playing.

All these "whys" for the time-out apply to FREEZE-FRAME. You could look at all the players of the team as a single energy unit, like the human body. When you regroup and FREEZE-FRAME in the heart, your entire system — glands, organs and nervous system — commences to work as a complete unit, yielding more available energy.

So let's discuss the steps to this time-out process. If you already practice a similar technique, read on anyway. You'll be able to appreciate the scientific verification and probably discover new applications from this technology.

Chapter Three

The Steps of FREEZE-FRAME

Here are the five steps of FREEZE-FRAME:

1. Recognize the stressful feeling, and FREEZE-FRAME it. *Take a time-out!*

2. Make a sincere effort to shift your focus away from the racing mind or disturbed emotions to the area around your heart. Pretend you're breathing through your heart to help focus your energy in this area. Keep your focus there for ten seconds or more.

3. Recall a positive fun feeling or time you've had in life and attempt to re-experience it.

4. Now, using your intuition, common sense, and sincerity — ask your heart, what would be a more efficient response to the situation, one that will minimize future stress?

5. Listen to what your heart says in answer to your question. (It's an effective way to put your reactive mind and emotions in check — and an "in-house" source of common sense solutions!)

Now let's explain these steps in more detail.

Step 1. **Recognize the stressful feeling, and FREEZE-FRAME it.** It's like pushing the pause button on your VCR. *Take a time-out!* This step helps you understand and recognize situations that you need to FREEZE-FRAME. Don't feel bad if at first you don't catch yourself until after the fact. "After the fact" is a whole lot better than not at all. Many people will process negative thoughts and feelings for hours, days, weeks, months, and longer. Acquiring the knowledge of how to shorten the duration of time you spend in all that unnecessary stress is what FREEZE-FRAME is about.

Step 2. **Make a sincere effort to shift your focus away from the racing mind or disturbed emotions to the area around your heart. Pretend you're breathing through your heart to help focus your energy in this area. Keep your focus there for ten seconds or more.** By shifting focus to the heart and away from the problem, you remove energy from your *perception* of the problem. This allows you to consider more effective possibilities. If you don't take time out for a moment or two, you'll never really be able to look at what is needed to make the most effective decision. Think about it this way. If you want to be the director of your own movie, you have to stop being just one of the characters and step back to see the whole picture.

Another way to look at it: If you're lost in the woods and panic and run smack into a tree, with your nose stuck right into the bark and your legs still running and digging into the ground, you're not going to get yourself out of the woods. So step back, FREEZE-FRAME and get a calm, objective look at the situation at hand. You will access a higher percentage of clarity. With clarity you can frame choices that you feel good about later. You also save energy and aging with this self-initiated effort.

When I say to focus your attention around the area of your heart, you might ask, is that just a convenient place to distract the mind or is there more to it? There's a lot more! We have always heard expressions like, "She speaks from the heart," "He played with all his heart." Being alive in the heart is what makes life worthwhile. In the enrichment of your heart feelings, you find your true core values. With heart guidance, quality decisions and real fun can be accessed. Heart-based decisions help move the mind into balance which results in effective action. The mind operating without the heart can create conveniences in the moment which generate stress later. It's the harmonious joint venture between the heart and mind that brings people quality experience in work, play and especially relationships.

By shifting focus to the inner heart, there's also benefit to the physical heart. Relieving strain on the physical heart caused by stress allows it to operate at greater efficiency. (See Chapter Four for information on how FREEZE-FRAME can boost cardiovascular efficiency.) Calming the heart rhythm in this way also helps activate a neuro-chemical communication pathway from the heart to the brain, reducing chaos in the mind and emotions. This causes the heart, mind/brain to work in a joint venture producing economy in energy expenditures.

Step 3. **Recall a positive fun feeling or time you've had in life and attempt to re-experience it.** Try to recall a positive episode you've had in life. This could be a fun vacation, a relationship experience, a time in nature, with children, etc. Remember how you *felt*. You might have felt appreciation, care, compassion or love. In the lab it's been shown that experiencing these positive feelings provides regeneration to the immune system, facilitating health and well-being. And they can assist us in seeing the world with more clarity and discernment.

Experiencing a positive feeling can be difficult at times, especially if the situation you are now in is extremely stressful and emotionally charged. *But the effort made to shift focus to a positive feeling like appreciation, whether from the past or in the present, helps you neutralize the negative reaction.* Becoming *neutral* in the face of stress is major progress. It facilitates hormonal balance, releasing the aggressive mental and emotional stress reactions. From neutral you have options on how to proceed. Even if you aren't able to experience feelings of appreciation, care or compassion, at least go for *neutral*. It helps take the stress monkey off your back by unclouding the mind and emotions. This keeps you from judging and reacting too quickly and paying the stress tax later.

The Power of Neutral

There is great power in learning to be neutral about issues until you have added awareness of the options. When you're neutral, you can adapt more quickly even if things don't go the way you'd wish. With a neutral attitude you don't waste energy prejudging a person or situation before you have a deeper comprehension of what is happening. Unfortunately, many people spend years worrying about the future, wasting tremendous energy. You lose the power to create a better future if you miss the opportunity of living in the "now."

Neutral is a conduit for objectivity in the moment. However, if you're unable to hold that objective position and find yourself right back in the heat of things, don't give up and think there's no hope. Be patient with yourself. Try to FREEZE-FRAME and find that neutral point again. A method to trigger hope is sticking with it and not panicking at the first difficulty. It's you whom you're taking care of now. If you were dealing with a couple of wild kids having a temper tantrum, would you just let them have their way because it was too hard to stop the noise? No, not if you loved them enough to want them to become responsible and balanced. So, back to yourself. If the emotions and racing mind don't just go away on command, try not to be impatient. Have some compassion for yourself just like you would with those children. Use understanding to harness that wild reactive energy one more time. Just FREEZE-FRAME. Each time you try, you exercise that muscle a little more. Then it gets fun to see your personal stress deficit being reduced daily.

Let's continue describing the steps of FREEZE-FRAME.

Step 4. **Now, using your intuition, common sense, and sincerity— ask your heart, what would be a more efficient response to the situation you are Freeze-Framing, one that will minimize future stress?** As you practice Freeze-Framing, your own intuition, common sense, and sincerity become more active and available. While you won't necessarily have crystal-clear revelations every time you FREEZE-FRAME, you can at least increase your capacity to arrive at convenient and practical solutions.

Step 5. **Listen to what your heart says in answer to your question.** The FREEZE-FRAME technique is simple, powerful, effective, and becomes automatic as you practice. Practice is not work, it's something that *works for you*. As you see the results, it becomes fun. Fun eats stress, just like "Pac Man."

So let's practice. Think of a current situation that's making you feel worried, anxious, impatient, frustrated, hopeless, etc. Go through the steps one at a time and try to find a new perspective that can reduce or prevent your stress.

Here are the steps again for quick reference:

1. **Recognize the stressful feeling, and FREEZE-FRAME it.**

2. **Make a sincere effort to shift your focus to the area around your heart. Pretend you're breathing through your heart to help focus your energy in this area. Keep your focus there for ten seconds or more.**

3. **Recall a positive fun feeling or time you've had in life and attempt to re-experience it.**

4. **Now, using your intuition, common sense, and sincerity — ask your heart, what would be a more efficient response to the situation, one that will minimize future stress?**

5. **Listen to what your heart says in answer to your question.**

Don't expect miracles or perfection. Skill is developed over time through sincere effort. It's the lack of sincerity that inhibits efforts from reaching their mark. Practicing FREEZE-FRAME is easier than you may think. It's something that people do naturally on occasion anyhow. The intelligence of pausing to take a deeper look before making decisions is already inherent within the heart of each person. FREEZE-FRAME is a simple technique to help you calm and manage the mind and emotions before making choices in day-to-day life. You'll learn to act from a point of balance, resulting in mental and emotional poise. This eliminates stress on contact and connects you with what your real self would think or do.

When I was learning to drive a car with a stick shift, before I got coordination between the clutch, brake, and accelerator pedal, I'd use the brake to slow down and stop the car without pressing the clutch. There was a lot of clunk and clank in my ride until I remembered to use the clutch. I realized I was putting a lot of strain on the car and creating embarrassing situations, like lurching out into the middle of an intersection while the stoplight was changing. FREEZE-FRAME is like putting the clutch in, allowing the flywheel (our emotions) to disengage, giving us options of shifting gears, using the brakes, or both. When we're in turmoil and attempt to set the brakes on our emotions, that suppresses them and places a lot of wear and tear on our system. FREEZE-FRAME helps you get off the accelerator. You don't have to shut the car off (or repress yourself — science has shown that's not good for you either). You just shift the car into neutral and balance out the emotions, allowing your mind to apprehend more fully what options you really have.

A Time Machine

How many times have you wished you could go back and change the way you handled or said something? But no matter how many times you replay the scene in your mind, you can't change it. It's in the past. All you can do is pick up the pieces and move on.

You can consider FREEZE-FRAME as a sort of time machine, one that can't take you back in time but helps wake you up **in the moment** so you can experience more quality time in the future. Think about all the energy you could save at work, with your family or any other aspect of your life, if you had the power to manage yourself **in the moment** when dealing with people, places or issues. Practicing FREEZE-FRAME facilitates being more conscious of your feelings and perceptions in the moment.

Freeze-Framing creates a time shift. How? By helping you to relinquish what you would have done and do that which would be *best for you* in a given situation. Your best option does not always result from your impulsive mental reactions and choices. These often create stress. When you make an efficient choice in moments of indecision, you establish more effectiveness within a time span, saving energy and stress. That's a time shift. Often our non-efficient choices can literally produce years of stress. That's a time loss. Sure, you can learn lessons from long drawn out stressful situations. However, a more beneficial thing to acknowledge is that you don't have to keep *learning* that way.

Practicing FREEZE-FRAME is utilizing practical preventive maintenance. It helps you unite with what your heart really knows rather than just following what your mind wants because you "can't help it," and later paying the dues. It's a common sense way of reducing stress and saving energy in your psychological system. It's the same type of common sense as using a crow bar to pull out nails rather than using your teeth. Much savings! Let's take a clean, clear look at the FREEZE-FRAME concept in action. Example:

You need a new car and have a strict budget — let's say $12,000. You go to the dealership already having picked a car within your budget, until you walk into the showroom. Lo and behold, you see the car of your dreams. It has enough bells and whistles that the original car you wanted now looks undernourished and wimpy. Suddenly, you are overwhelmed with mobile lust. Guess what? It's $30,000. Your *heart* says, "Not now, but maybe in a year or so." Your mind says, "I couldn't make the payments, but what if I gave up aerobics, eating out, designer underwear and my paid vacation (you'll take the pay but won't vacate)." Again your heart says, "Just say no!" But your mind is dazzled and victimized by the clutches of showroom glamour. Once again your heart says, "It would be too much of a stretch and stress to make payments." Then, appropriately, the dealer says, "If you take the expensive car, I'll knock $500 off the price." That did it! Justification. Like most people, you are addicted to buying anything you can get "on sale." You find yourself deciding to buy the "hunk." After all, it was on sale!

Friend, right then is when you could use the convenience of a FREEZE-FRAME. Why? Because your heart's intuitive common sense has already said "no" to the expensive model. Yet, your mind fell vulnerable to the glitter. (And a sale!) A FREEZE-FRAME could be your last chance to steer your mind back into the real world. You could save those years of extra stress and aging by not buying the showroom hunk until you were financially able to afford it. The novelty of that expensive car will likely wear off in two months at the most. However, those stretching payments and the accompanying stress can go on and on and on. Discover FREEZE-FRAME and give yourself a last chance to listen to your heart before you engage in an unnecessary stressful commitment. You can preserve your mental and emotional health and peace by preventing these types of impulses.

This is just a graphic example of the convenience of a FREEZE-FRAME. I'm sure you can backtrack and consider similar situations in your past — times when just *one* FREEZE-FRAME could have provided you that extra deeper insight before you leaped into a decision which brought you months or even years of repeated stress. This story illustrates the inner self-talk we often have. Practicing FREEZE-FRAME regularly helps you remember to use the technique at major decision-making crossroads.

I could tell you story after story about myself, when I reacted too quickly, without inner poise or clarity. The taxes I paid on those non-efficient reactions motivated me to find an internal decision-making tool that could bring me clarity before acting. In searching for such a tool, I had to take a closer look at how I arrived at decisions. I saw that there were two aspects of myself repeatedly in conflict — which I termed the head and the heart. There had to be an avenue for balancing my mental (or emotional) impulses with my core intuitive feelings. I experienced those core feelings here and there, and noticed they seemed to bring the clarity I needed. I wanted to understand the inner mechanics of my head and heart so I could regularly access that core intuition. Through observing my inner self-talk, I saw that when I could really calm my head thoughts and emotions, then my core intuitive feelings became more clear. I began to develop the technique of FREEZE-FRAME and taught the steps to others to see if they'd have the same results. When they did, I decided to scientifically research what was occurring in the heart and brain while someone Freeze-Framed. Since people also reported improved health after regularly practicing FREEZE-FRAME, the scientists I was working with wanted to test what effect this technique was having on the immune system as well. The results were surprising and especially encouraging. FREEZE-FRAME proved to be a simple technique that puts the heart, mind, brain and emotions in a resonant state, creating the inner atmosphere for intuitive clarity.

Let's take a look at the scientific basis for FREEZE-FRAME.

Chapter Four

The Scientific Basis of the FREEZE-FRAME Technology

FREEZE-FRAME is a tool whose effectiveness has been scientifically proven in a variety of research studies. The implications of this research are profound. People have long searched for a pill, drug or device that would give them better health or happiness. In the USA, eight of the ten top-selling prescription drugs are for stress-related problems[1], such as ulcers, hypertension, depression, and anxiety. Science is proving that dependency on these drugs can lead to additional stress from side effects or addiction. It's important to realize that the flourishing sales of these prescription drugs are dwarfed by astronomical sales of illegal drugs that millions take in the pursuit of feeling better — drugs like cocaine, heroin, and crack.

According to the Mayo Clinic, in the past decade cardiovascular fitness has become synonomous with good health. New research studies on the heart are being released at a rapid rate. The Research Division of the Institute of HeartMath (IHM) is engaged in several areas of investigation seeking to correlate mental and emotional attitudes, the heart's electrical system, and the immune system. This research is proving what many of us already know intuitively — that our mental and emotional attitudes are directly related to the health of our heart, our immune system, and our happiness.

The Role of the Heart

In addition to being an efficient pump supplying blood to our entire body, the heart is also our main power center. Electrically, it is 40 to 60 times more powerful than the brain, supplying 2.5 watts of electrical power. The heartbeat, which produces an electrical signal, can be measured at any point on the body. A doctor could place electrodes on your ear lobes, little toe, or anywhere on your body and record your electrocardiogram (ECG) signal. So, quite literally, the electrical signal from the heart permeates every cell.

Heart Rate Variability — A Key Measure of Mental and Emotional Balance

If you go to a doctor's office for a physical exam, you may be told your heart is beating at 70 beats per minute. This is an average figure because the time intervals between heartbeats are always changing. Heart rate variability (HRV) is a measure of these beat-to-beat changes in heart rate as the heart speeds up and slows down in different patterns. These heart rate changes are influenced by almost any stimulus the brain and mind process, such as emotions, thoughts, sound, light, etc.

There is a two-way communication between the heart and the brain that regulates heart rate and blood pressure[2]. Analysis of HRV is used by doctors to measure the balance between the sympathetic and parasympathetic nervous systems, two important components of this communication system. Our perceptions and emotional reactions are transmitted between the heart and brain via these nervous systems and can be seen in the patterns of our heart rhythms[3].

The graph in Figure A(1) on page 41 shows the typical HRV pattern of someone feeling frustrated or edgy. When you feel edgy inside, you are likely to experience this type of heart rhythm. This excess wear and tear can create a chain reaction in your body. For example, when you're frustrated your nervous system is out of balance, your blood vessels constrict, blood pressure rises, and you waste a lot of energy. If this happens consistently, you can become hypertensive and greatly increase your risk of heart disease. Hypertensive individuals are two to three times more likely to develop coronary artery disease and four times more likely to suffer a stroke. As you've already read, it's estimated that one in four Americans, approximately 60 million people, are hypertensive. Heart disease now accounts for slightly more than 50% of all deaths reported in the U.S.[4]

On the other hand, feelings of sincere appreciation create the HRV pattern you see in Figure A(2), which is a smooth, even rhythm. This pattern is an example of cardiovascular efficiency. What's happening is that the two nervous systems are "entraining" and working together at maximum efficiency instead of fighting each other. Think of entrainment as being "in sync." When your head and heart, thoughts and feelings, are working harmoniously together, you have more clarity and inner balance — and you feel better.

Figure A(1) — Stress-Producing Heart Rhythm

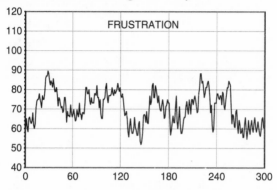

Figure A(2) — Harmonious Heart Rhythm

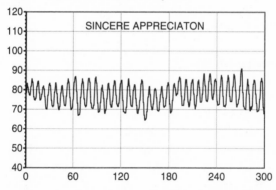

Figure A illustrates the heart rate variability pattern of frustration (top) which is characterized by its random, jerky pattern. Deep sincere feeling states like appreciation (bottom) can result in ordered HRV patterns, generally associated with efficient cardiovascular function. This pattern is an example of what scientists call *entrainment*, in which the sympathetic and parasympathetic nervous systems are working together efficiently.

There is a third nerve pathway involved in the heart/mind/brain communication link, called the Baroreceptor system (see Figure B on page 43). This pathway originates in the heart, sends information to the brain, and can affect perception. This is the only pathway known that, when stimulated, communicates to the higher brain centers where learning takes place. IHM research shows that the FREEZE-FRAME process of focusing attention in the area of the heart while experiencing a positive feeling activates this pathway. This may explain the shift in perception experienced after Freeze-Framing.

Heart rate variability is an excellent measure of nervous system balance, and research is showing that our perceptions and reactions affect our heart rhythms. Therefore, heart rate variability is an important indication of how well we are balancing our lives. As you become practiced in FREEZE-FRAME, you can balance your nervous systems and change your heart rhythm patterns *in the moment*, as shown in Figure C (page 44).

Electrocardiogram Analysis

Besides looking at heart rate variability patterns, doctors also analyze electrocardiograms (ECG) to determine the health of the physical heart. For some years, scientists have been able to see the effects of hostility[5] and severe depression in the ECG[6]. Only recently, through the use of ECG spectral analysis, have they been able to see the effects of even more subtle "negative" emotions, such as frustration, worry, and anxiety, as well as the effects of "positive" emotions such as love, care, compassion, and appreciation.

It is probably no coincidence that the electrical pattern of frustration in the chart on page 45 looks about like it feels. When life is crashing down around you — your boss is yelling, pressure is mounting, the phone is

Figure B — Heart-Brain Communication System

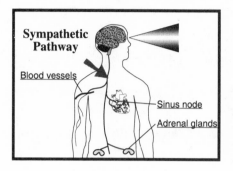

The sympathetic branch of the autonomic nervous system is like a biological wire that carries electrical impulses from the brain to the heart, adrenal glands, blood vessels, and other parts of the body. Its role is to speed up these systems. How active it is, is based on our perceptions.

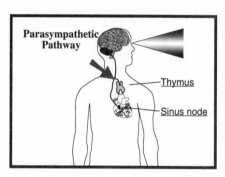

The parasympathetic branch of the nervous system has the opposite role of the sympathetic, and acts to slow down or cool down the heart and other organs. Balance between both branches is essential for overall health.

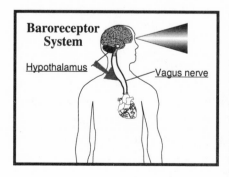

This pathway — the baroreceptor system — transmits electrical information from the heart to the brain, allowing for two-way communication. This is the only known nerve pathway which, when stimulated, can alter perception in the higher brain centers.

Figure C — Physiological Benefits of FREEZE-FRAME

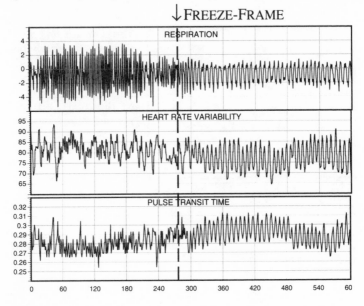

Figure C illustrates the change in respiration, heart rate and blood pressure (pulse transit time) when this person Freeze-Framed, which occurred near the 300 sec. mark on the graph. Pulse transit time is a way of measuring blood pressure on a (heart) beat-to-beat basis. Notice how all three variables have nearly identical patterns — they have "entrained" and are in harmony with each other. (The bottom graph is inverted, meaning higher time values equal lower blood pressure.)

ringing, the copier is jammed and you're frustrated — your ECG spectra is likely to look like the top graph of Figure D(1) on page 45. This is called an "incoherent spectrum" and you probably *feel* pretty incoherent when life is falling apart. At other times, if your boss has just sincerely thanked you for a job well done, or you have a productive meeting with a co-worker, or when you love what you're doing and feel appreciation for life, your ECG probably looks more like the harmonious pattern of Figure D(2), called a "coherent spectrum." At these moments, life is going your way and you feel more coherent — you have more clarity and balance. Feelings of love, care, or compassion can all lead to a more coherent ECG spectrum, similar to the graph of appreciation. On the other hand, research has found that feelings of anger, anxiety, irritation, or resentment all produce incoherent spectra that look similar to the graph of frustration. Remember, this electrical energy is being radiated to every cell in your body.

Figure D(1) — ECG: Incoherent Spectrum

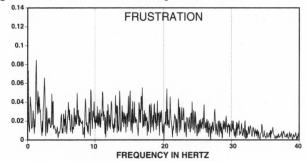

Figure D(2) — ECG: Coherent Spectrum

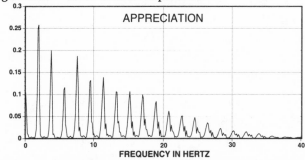

Figure D shows the spectrum analysis of eight seconds of ECG data while feeling frustrated (top) and while feeling sincere appreciation (bottom). Notice the greatly increased order and power in the spectrum while appreciation was experienced. Spectrum analysis shows the individual frequencies that create the complex ECG wave that permeates every cell in the body.

How Your Heart Affects Others

The electrical waves of the heart are like radio waves in that they are transmitted outside of us as well as to every cell of our body. This may explain why you can sometimes walk into a room and tell if two people just had an argument, even though they are quietly standing there. You can feel it in the air. The electrical frequencies radiated by the heart change dramatically when we are in different emotional states and can affect not only ourselves but the people around us. By learning to create internal entrainment and coherence through the FREEZE-FRAME process, we radiate a much more harmonious signal to our environment.

"Beyond 2000" — Freeze-Framing in Action

In late 1993, a videotape crew from the television program "Beyond 2000," came to the Institute's research facility to do a feature on the music *Heart Zones**, which I designed scientifically to help people achieve more mental and emotional balance and renewed vitality. The crew wanted to understand how the music was created and how we were able to prove its effectiveness in our laboratory research.

The host for the show decided to open the segment by being hooked up to all the physiological testing equipment in the lab — heart rate, ECG, EEG (brain waves), blood pressure, respiration, and more. Computers tracked all his physiological responses as he was videotaped. Unfortunately, he stumbled over his opening lines several

---

* *Heart Zones* spent 50 weeks on the Billboard charts, and is being used in a wide variety of business and personal applications. See page 134 for more information.

times, forcing repeated 'takes' and he became increasingly tense and nervous. The computers showed the results of his mounting tension. His blood pressure and heart rate had shot up to extremely high levels. The scientist monitoring the host's physiological responses suggested he try the FREEZE-FRAME technique he had learned earlier. As you can see in Figure E, within seconds his heart rate and blood pressure returned to normal, and his respiration regained a smooth even pattern. He then delivered his lines perfectly. The host and crew were delighted that they had real-time verification of FREEZE-FRAME's effectiveness captured on videotape.

Figure E

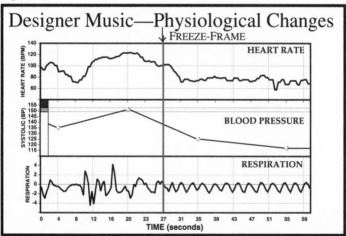

Figure E. Chart shows the effect of *Heart Zones* and FREEZE-FRAME on an individual with little prior training. The individual was the host of the TV show *Beyond 2000* featured on the Discovery Channel.

How Your Heart Affects Your Hormones and Immune System

Let's look at more scientific facts on the relationship between emotions and health. Scientists are proving that repeated episodes of anger and frustration cause nervous system imbalances that are detrimental not only to the heart, but to the brain and the hormonal and immune systems. Have you ever had a big argument with some-one you loved and, the next day, replayed the situation over and over in your mind, cranking up negative emotions from the day before that made you feel terrible? Even recalling an upsetting episode can produce imbalances and stress. As mentioned earlier, we know that stress creates specific hormonal imbalances, and that these same hormonal imbalances have been shown to damage brain cells. They may even lead to Alzheimer's disease[7]. It doesn't have to be that way once you understand what you are doing to yourself and how you can change it.

Studies show that feelings of happiness and joy increase white blood cell counts needed for healing[8] and defend against invading pathogens, including cancer and virus-infected cells.

The Immune System's First Defender

IgA (immunoglobulin A) is an immune system antibody and one of the body's first lines of defense against colds, flu, and infections of the respiratory and urinary tracts. IgA is found in our saliva, blood, lungs, digestive and urinary systems. In a group study (twenty individuals) comparing the effects of anger versus care and compassion on average IgA levels, it was found that one five-minute episode of mentally and emotionally recalling an experience of anger and frustration caused an immediate but short rise in IgA, followed by a depletion that was so severe it took the body more than six hours to restore normal production of IgA (see Figure F(1) on page 50). What this study showed is that even a single episode of *recalling* an experience of anger and frustration can depress your immune system for almost an entire day[9].

What are most people's days like? You wake up anxious because you didn't sleep well; you get frustrated with a co-worker who forgot to give you an important report; somebody gives you a strange look at the coffee machine and you feel a surge of irritation. Then you find 15 voice-mail messages that you're late responding to — it's a cascading series of events of anxiety, frustration and anger. The cumulative results of seemingly insignificant frustrations and anxieties have been shown to be even more detrimental to the immune system than the occasional large blow-out of anger[10]. Is it any wonder that health care costs are so high, eating up a huge percentage of corporate profits and expected to get worse?

This same IgA study also showed that one five-minute episode of mentally and emotionally experiencing the emotions of care and compassion caused a much larger, immediate rise in IgA — an average of 34% — followed by a return to normal (baseline)[9]. However, the IgA levels then gradually climbed above baseline throughout the next six hours (see Figure F(2)). With today's hectic lifestyle, how many of us have more enjoyable experiences of care, fun or passion for life than we do anger or frustration on any given day? Learning to manage the moment and increase the ratio of our positive attitudes and feelings can improve our quality of life and well-being.

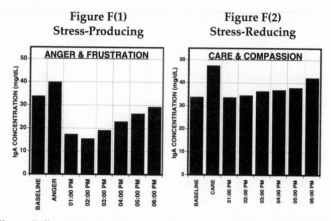

Figure F(1)
Stress-Producing

Figure F(2)
Stress-Reducing

Figure F illustrates the effect that feeling care and compassion (right) had on the experimental group's average IgA levels throughout the day. There was an immediate and significant increase in IgA, and while it dropped back to normal an hour later, IgA levels continued to increase throughout the rest of the day. Individuals experiencing a 5-minute period of anger and frustration (left) had an immediate increase in IgA. However, a dramatic decrease in IgA levels followed, and lasted throughout the day, showing the powerful effects even one episode of recalling an experience of anger can have on the immune system. This may explain why some people say they "feel better" after blowing their top. But they pay a day-long price later on.

FREEZE-FRAME with HIV-positive/AIDS patients

In a study using FREEZE-FRAME with HIV-positive and AIDS patients, researchers found dramatic improvements in anxiety levels and physical symptoms. Using the STAI (State Trait Anxiety Inventory) to measure psychological changes, participants who practiced FREEZE-FRAME for six months tremendously reduced their level of despair, anger, fear and guilt. At the beginning of the study, most of the participants had severe anxiety disorders — understandable considering the condition of their health and the general prognosis for people diagnosed HIV-positive. By the end of the six-month study, average anxiety levels had dropped by 20%, almost to that of the average healthy person, in spite of the fact that they still had a virus that is feared by society and could supposedly kill them at any time[11]. They experienced more balance and harmonious flow throughout the day. More things seemed to go their way, and they were able to increase the percentage of these good days and get more done.

Here is a comment from one of the participants:

"[FREEZE-FRAME] has empowered me to focus on what is truly important in my life. So much of my time has been spent dwelling on what poor decisions I made or how I didn't measure up to expectations. Now I have the ability to choose a happier, healthier emotion to get me through situations of despair or remorse. Each day brings me so much joy and opportunities to appreciate all that is around me — family, friends, and life are so precious. If this is all there is, I am choosing to make it the most pleasant, rich, and happy experience possible and HeartMath has given me the ability to make these choices."

Affiliative Motive

Let's look at another psychological measure, the "affiliative motive." Affiliation is a social motive characterized by the desire to establish warm and caring relationships with others. People with strong affiliative motive tend to be loving and caring individuals. It has been shown that loving and caring people have decreased levels of stress hormones, and higher IgA levels during times of stress than non-affiliative individuals[12]. They get sick less often and are less vulnerable to disease[13]. Loving and caring people also have increased norepinephrine, a chemical released from the nerves that has a wide variety of functions in balancing the nervous systems[14]. Studies have shown that even if you aren't naturally affiliative, self-induced feelings of warmth and care towards others also increase IgA levels[15], resulting in an enhanced immune system.

Easy Access

The FREEZE-FRAME technology focuses your attention in the area around the heart (where people subjectively feel love, care, appreciation, etc.). These feelings have been shown to help balance the nervous systems. When you FREEZE-FRAME, an electrical signal is triggered in the perceptual center in the brain via another set of nerves which lead from the heart to the brain. This helps to give you a more balanced perspective of any situation.

FREEZE-FRAME is a technology that gives you the conscious ability to self-manage your reactions, gain clarity and have more quality, fun and well-being in the moment. You gain the power to make better choices and decisions and not be victimized by your reactions to people, places and situations. Just as the detrimental effects of stress are cumulative, so are the beneficial effects of FREEZE-FRAME. Practice leads to increased mental and emotional buoyancy, cardiovascular efficiency and improved quality of life. Here's how it works inside our body (see flow chart on next page).

Your perceptions trigger your mental and emotional responses, which cause electrical changes in the nervous

```
┌─────────────────────────────────────────┐
│              PERCEPTION                   │
└─────────────────────────────────────────┘
                    ▼
┌─────────────────────────────────────────┐
│        MENTAL AND EMOTIONAL               │
│             RESPONSE                      │
└─────────────────────────────────────────┘
                    ▼
┌─────────────────────────────────────────┐
│    ELECTRICAL CHANGES IN HEART            │
│      AND NERVOUS SYSTEM                    │
└─────────────────────────────────────────┘
                    ▼
┌─────────────────────────────────────────┐
│        HORMONE AND IMMUNE                 │
│          SYSTEM CHANGES                   │
└─────────────────────────────────────────┘
                    ▼
┌─────────────────────────────────────────┐
│   POSITIVE OR NEGATIVE EFFECTS            │
│    Physical Energy, Mental Clarity,       │
│  Emotional Balance, Personal Effectiveness│
└─────────────────────────────────────────┘
```

system, heart and brain. Those electrical changes directly affect your heart rate, blood pressure, hormonal and immune responses, which in turn influence health and aging. These changes result in physical energy or depletion, mental and emotional clarity or the lack of it, whether you relate well to others or not, and how well you relate to yourself. This cascade of events determines your behavior, which affects your next perception, and the cycle continues. As you practice FREEZE-FRAME you will gain a higher ratio of positive to negative effects on your health and well-being.

Learning to manage the moment can literally change the quality of your life.

References

1. American Druggist, February 1994
2. M. Levey, and P. Martin: Autonomic Control of Cardiac Function, in Physiology and Pathophysiology of the Heart, second edition (1989)
3. R. McCraty, M. Atkinson, and W. Tiller: New Electro-physiological Correlates of Mental & Emotional States via Heart Rate Variability Studies, PROC. ISSSEEM 1994 Conference, Boulder, CO (1994)
4. J. Lynch: The Language of the Heart, Basic Books, New York
5. R. Williams: Anger Kills, Times Books, New York
6. V.K. Yeragani, R. Pohl, R. Balon, C. Ramesh, D. Glitz, I. Jung and P. Sherwood: Heart Rate Variability in Patients with Major Depression, Psychiatry Research 37 (1991) 35
7. D. Kerr, L. Campbell, M. Applegate, A. Brodish, and P. Landfeild: Chronic Stress-induced Acceleration of Electrophysiologic and Morphometric Biomarkers of Hippocampal Aging, Journal of Neuroscience, 11 May (1991) 1316
8. R. Zachariae, P. Bjerring, C. Zachariae, L. Arendt-Nielsen, T. Nielsen, E. Eldrup, C. Schade Larsen, K. Gotliebsen: Monocyte chemotactic activity in sera after hypnotically induced emotional states. Scan J Immunol 34 (1991) 71-79,
9. G. Rein and R. McCraty: Long Term Effects of Compas-sion and Anger on Salivary IgA, Psychosomatic Medicine 54 (1994) 171
10. L. Jandorf, E. Deblinger, M. Neale, A. Stone: Daily vs Major Life Events as Predictors of Symptom Frequency: A Replication Study, Journal of General Psychology 113 (1986) 205
11. D. Rozman, R. Whitaker, T. Beckman, D. Jones: Initial Use of a New Intervention Program for Significantly Reduc-ing Psychological Symptomatology in HIV Seropositive Individuals

12. D.C. McClelland, G. Ross, V. Patel: The effect of an academic examination on salivary norepinephrine and immunoglobulin levels. J Human Stress 11 (1985) 52-59
13. D.C. McClelland, J.B. Jemmott: Power motivation, stress and physical illness. J Human Stress 6 (1980) 6-15,
14. J.B. Jemmott, J.Z. Borysenko, M. Borysenko, D.C. McClelland, R. Chapman, D. Meyed, H. Benson: Academic stress, power motivation and decrease in salivary secretory immunoglobulin A secretion rate. Lancet 1 (1983) 1400
15. D.C. McClelland, C. Kirshnit: The effect of motivational arousal through films on salivary immunoglobulin A. Psychol and Health 2 (1988) 31-52

Chapter Five

Personal Benefits and Applications

Now that you know some of the physiological and health implications of learning to FREEZE-FRAME, and are ready to begin, let's review one of the most important points. Remember, your objective at this stage of the game is to reach a certain level of *neutral*. Neutral is the safe zone, the place where thoughts and concerns come to rest for a moment or two so you can gain that new level of clarity. In a time of confusion or indecision, how many people do you know who are able to find a wider perspective that is helpful and non-stress-producing? Neutral is the place where you find that higher ground. It's like finding the balance point on a seesaw and holding steady between up and down. Being able to do this consistently builds emotional control and inner power.

Emotional control from the heart is the first step to neutral. That's what clears the static from the computer screen of your mind to present you a window through which to see clearly. Otherwise, your mind can seem like a computer with a distorted screen or no screen at all. Freeze-Framing gives you the option to "re-frame" what's on the screen before it starts a deficit. In that moment, you have the opportunity to create a time shift, resulting in immediate and future energy-saving outcomes.

Once you recognize you want to end your stress, take "time out" to FREEZE-FRAME. Then quiet the mind and cool down the emotions by remembering the value of inner balance. That's the time to find and hold the neutral zone. Again, neutral is neutral. It's not up or down, good or bad, right or wrong. It's more like wait and see. If you've ever heard two people arguing over opposing opinions, I'll bet your instincts said if they both would pause to take a sincere look they'd be more likely to untangle the mess they'd created. If you can see that in others, wouldn't you want to be aware of that process in yourself?

FREEZE-FRAME is like that friend who helps you recognize the need to step back. And a convenient friend at that, being centrally located right in your own heart, just one "stop" away from the head. The sole requirement is to remember to call for help. It's a power tool waiting to be used.

Let's go back to neutral. Reflect on all the positives, the benefits of neutral — the degenerative hormones that don't flow through your system, the nerves that don't have to fry, the cells that don't age as quickly, the heart that doesn't have to strain. Award yourself the credit you deserve for becoming neutral. It's the first sign that the inner muscle is responding and starting to flex. You've taken a giant step forward in building your personal power.

The next step is to explore the benefits of using FREEZE-FRAME in specific areas of life — at work and within yourself — mentally, emotionally and physically. In each section, you can check your stress levels in that area and see how Freeze-Framing has helped people in similar situations.

THE BUSINESS BENEFITS

Effectiveness in business requires mental skills to shape accurate and fast decisions. Increasingly, business is becoming "lean and mean." This translates as more pressure, longer work hours, increased responsibility and the need to adapt quickly to change. For most, the threat of corporate down-sizing is present as well. These external pressures, combined with a lack of mental and emotional self-management, can result in the slow burn of accelerating stress. Yet, as the statistics in Chapter One show, people are unaware of the seriousness of their inner stress until they come to the end of their rope — in mental, emotional or physical burnout.

A large majority of business people we work with say they wait all year for a one or two week vacation to escape from stress, only to discover that the stress travels with them. Just getting away from the job and the usual routine can be stressful. Then for the first few days of the vacation, it's hard to turn off the mind and unwind. For the next several days they begin to feel like they're on vacation. But as the vacation draws to a close, problems at the office or at home start to intrude again in their thoughts. The last few days they're restless with these concerns. When they return to work they wonder what happened to their vacation. Freeze-Framing won't extend your vacation or necessarily change the demands of your job, but it can release a lot of the built-up pressure and increase the enjoyment of your holiday. Whether you are in sales, customer service, factory work, administration, etc., you can probably think of obvious opportunities to try out Freeze-Framing. As you experience for yourself how fast this simple, powerful tool releases stress on the inside, you'll find it a work tool as essential as your daily planner, calculator or computer. So let's take a business stress check.

Which of these business-related stresses apply to you?

❑ Overloaded with deadlines, always rushed?

❑ Communication conflicts with co-workers?

❑ Need stress or pressure to get the job done?

❑ Unappreciated for my efforts?

❑ Consumed by work issues after hours?

❑ Job insecurity?

❑ "Overcaring " — getting close to burnout?

❑ Other?_____

Business today is so fast-moving, it takes tremendous energy to *keep* up and not get *eaten* up. Business usually signifies head thoughts, head decisions, head all day long, often winding up with a head *ache*. People feel like computers — always organizing, analyzing, sorting data at high speed. To have the smoothest-running head possible for your job, wouldn't a little cleaning be good for the disk drive? Freeze-Framing is designed to supply that regular cleaning required for clear-headed decision-making.

Business needs more heart. I could cite statistic after statistic of how many people in business feel treated like cogs, not people, of how un-cared for they feel, and how unmotivated and unproductive they are as a result. One in three Americans seriously thought about quitting work in 1990 because of chronic job stress, and one in three expects to 'burn out' on the job in the near future. Business is changing rapidly, and it's harder and harder to stay competitive. Companies that treat people better and put heart in what they do will have the real competitive advantage in the future. (They already do.) Business guru, Tom Peters, author of the books *In Search of Excellence* and *Liberation Management*, seems to agree:

"Store shelves groan under the weight of new products, but few have heart. Service offerings are about as lifeless. Most hotels, for example, spent the last decade buffing their customer service. The mechanics are better. Bravo. But the heart is usually absent: the sincere sense of 'Welcome to my home' as opposed to 'I've gotta remember to act like I care.'"

It's the lack of heart that's gotten business where it is today, with more stress and anxiety than ever. People are frying by the truckloads. Every day countless numbers hate to go to work; their hearts are not there. FREEZE-FRAME activates the power of your heart to guide you in directions where business can become more successful and satisfying.

Balanced Care Vs. Overcare

When I say business demands more care, some people would protest, "But I *do* care. It's because I care so much that I'm worn out." People do care that the job gets done, that the company achieves its sales goal, that their share price rises, and so forth. When "care" starts to deplete you, it's become "overcare." Overcare is one of the most consequential energy drains in the human system. It keeps you from enjoying and profiting from the things you *care* about. Most people assume it's the heart's intentions that cause overcare. It's not! The unmanaged mind puts people into overcare. The heart cares, but it's the mind that causes the worry and anxiety resulting in overcare and depletion. This creates constant low grade stress and can eventually lead to burnout. Even if you don't reach the point of burnout, life can still feel like you're flying on a plane with one engine out — living at a low quality level with a lack of fulfillment.

Balanced care is regenerating. As you've read in Chapter Four, feelings of care induce harmonious, coherent heart rhythms which balance the nervous system, enhance the immune response and help mental clarity. Overcare — feeling worried, anxious or frustrated in the name of care — causes stress-producing heart rhythms, creating out-of-sync signals between the heart and brain, impairing decision-making ability, lowering the immune response and your personal energy level as well.

Overcare about children, jobs, traffic, sports, pets, relationships, life, etc., occupies tremendous amounts of people's energy throughout the business day and at home. The blanket word for accumulated overcare is "worry." Worry is overcare in continuous motion, a vampire of emotional health and well-being. It's like a social predator that preys on the mental and emotional nature, producing serious energy drains both in individuals and in the collective environment. The deceptive aspect of overcare is that it can always be justified by the mind. People are especially prone to justify overcaring in relationships and job issues. They frequently damage themselves far more from overcare than they would if they lost the relationship or the job. Worry and overcare seem natural, but they're really "hand-me-down" stressor patterns from uneducated social belief systems. A little worry is hard to prevent at times, but with practice you can minimize it and save your health and happiness. Science has already proven that worry takes its toll. Take it out of your diet plan; it's loaded with additives. I know from experience.

Overcare in relationships leads to attachments that smother people's spirits and eventually alienate those with whom you are trying to get closer. Care for people, but don't put a noose around them. That just creates emotional luggage which drags them down until, finally, for self-preservation, they free themselves from that luggage and release their spirit to enjoy life again. Simply said, unbalanced care for people prevents them from being themselves. People don't like that. You don't. Freeze-Framing helps you become more conscious of energy drains from overcare.

Overcare occurs when there is mental or emotional over-identity with people, opinions, attitudes, issues, results, etc. People often recognize the energy depletion and strike out in anger at others or become angry with themselves for being victimized by their own overdoing. Still, due to lack of self-management, they continue the overcare, accumulating further stress while staying trapped in that same feedback loop. For example, after company meetings, a line manager often would become downright mad about the way something was said or done at the meeting. He'd stay mad for hours thinking about it and mad at himself for not having spoken up during the meeting. Caught in an inner feedback loop, he'd then blame his self-created anger on the meeting — how unfocused it was, the time wasted — and, finally, on the company. Much business stress is created by people's reactions to meetings, when it's their own overcare that keeps them from speaking up. Then later they feel victimized. Freeze-Framing during meetings can help you stop, think deeper, and realize that you can calmly speak your truth in the moment and learn to cut corners. Think of all the time and energy wasted, and business opportunities lost, when people stay angry at others or at themselves, replaying what they should have said or done — a no-win situation that accumulates ongoing stress in the workplace.

Overcare can be a hard momentum to reverse. Preventive maintenance would be a wise energy investment. How do you know if overcare is sapping your vitality? Look at the people and issues you care about. Is your caring in a given area causing stress? If you find yourself feeling drained because of care, that's an excellent time to FREEZE-FRAME the situation and take a deeper look to see if it's overcare rather than care. While Freeze-Framing, ask yourself, "Is my caring helpful for myself and others? Or is it draining both myself and others?" Remember, balanced care is regenerative; overcare is depleting. If you're honest with yourself, your heart intuition and common sense will broaden the perspective and assist you in attaining balanced care.

For example, if you over-push a sale in desperation to close it, you can often drive the client right into your competitor's arms. Freeze-Framing helps you to regulate and balance your sales savvy without distasteful aggression. This can increase your rate of closure.

It takes a little practice to observe and understand the fine line between care and overcare. If you're in a traffic jam and late for a business meeting, it's okay to care about it. However, if you don't balance that care it crosses into anxiety, dilutes your energy reserve and can even wreck the rest of your day. Freeze-Framing hands you a chance to put your outgoing energies of overcare in check now, in order to save pain and stress "backwash" later. Observe yourself for a week in areas of life that you care about. See if you are manufacturing more stress for yourself or others due to overcare. I think you'll discover this exercise to be fun, interesting and potentially profitable. After you intercept your overcare, then Freeze-Framing will afford you a *choice* in the moment to prevent an overdraw on your energy account. Peace and quality of life depend on how wisely people spend their energies day-to-day. Why sleep at night to recharge if you're going to squander the energy the next day through mismanagement?

Transforming Stress into Creative Energy

Many believe that stress is a necessary motivator for business success. If adrenaline isn't constantly pumping through them, and everyone else, they think the job won't get done. It's critical to know the difference between what I call *creative resistance*, which recharges your batteries, and the stress that drains and ages you. As science has shown, stress releases hormones that can be energizing and fun in the moment, but can also deplete and damage the human system. Via Freeze-Framing, you maintain balance while you exert yourself — and know when to stop. It's *fun stress*, like stretching yourself to jog that extra mile without pushing yourself over the edge. Your nervous system remains in balance, releasing regenerative hormones throughout your body and turning stress into available, productive energy.

To be able to think on your feet with both your heart and your head alleviates considerable stress. Remember, your goal is to create balance in the two-way communication system between your heart and your brain. This leads to a greater ratio of peace over stress and much more fun. In the future people will understand that giving attention to overcare and stress is at the hub of better business. Attention to these areas is the foundation of business effectiveness and will lead to greater harmony between business and people.

In business today you can't FREEZE-FRAME too often. You can utilize it at every turn — when you're feeling rushed or overloaded; in the middle of a communication conflict; when you're overcaring about a client or the impending quarterly financial report; when your boss ignores your sincere efforts *again*; when thoughts about work keep consuming you at home or with your family; and especially if you're feeling burned out. Many of the external issues in business that cause stress will not change overnight, but each time you shift your perspective you achieve more personal power to adapt and come out ahead. With usage, Freeze-Framing becomes automatic and a way of life. It will help you *adapt* to what you *can't* change and show you what you *can* change. It feels good to experience the flex of your own empowerment and keeps your system filled with hope.

Allow me to relate several examples I've been told of how FREEZE-FRAME has transformed communication stress, sales stress, and organizational stress into creative assets.

Turning a Wasted Call into New Business

A prominent Canadian entrepreneur owns a company that provides outplacement services to corporations and to individuals. He was due to meet with a large governmental agency that was downsizing. He had been warned it would be extremely challenging to communicate with the woman he would be meeting and that their talk would probably be a waste of time. As the session began, he realized the advice had been accurate. Instead of overcaring and trying to make his sales pitch as soon as she took a breath, he decided to FREEZE-FRAME, stay neutral, and just listen to the woman. Throughout the appointment he listened sincerely to her concerns, without judging her for her gruff and "know it all" style. At the conclusion of the meeting, the woman was so impressed with his sensitivity and with being heard, she agreed to do business with his firm and personally introduce him to influential decision-makers in the government.

Can you see the sequence of events here? It's a psychological equation that's been proven to work:

Difficult clients + FREEZE-FRAME = Clarity and non-identity with negative reactions = Sensitive listening to clients' real needs = Higher potential of closing the sale

---

Managing a Global Project Effectively

A multi-billion dollar Silicon Valley corporation recently decided to open 16 new videoconferencing facilities world-wide. The corporation was already quite pleased with the efficiency and cost-effectiveness of its 12 sites and was eager to expand rapidly. However, the videoconference manager felt concerned by the prospect of managing this massive global project, implementing new standards of technology with a high risk factor, and gaining the close cooperation of at least six vendors, her own team, and senior management. Having been trained in FREEZE-FRAME through our *Inner Quality Management®* (IQM) program, she Freeze-Framed and came up with a solution to ensure the success of this project: Provide an IQM training in FREEZE-FRAME to all the key people involved, so they could work collectively and communicate with more effectiveness. She envisioned that convening all these people at one time for in-depth planning would conserve a tremendous amount of time, energy, and money. After the training, the manager commented that not only were the people working together better than ever before, but they accomplished in *two days* what could easily have taken *months!*

Communication conflicts between co-workers cause some of the biggest energy deficits in business. When communications are just head to head, they are likely to result in blame and backbiting — like magnets repelling each other. When communications are heart-based and sincere, the result is more like magnets pulling together to increase cooperation and team building.

Overcoming Conflict with a Boss

For the new marketing director of a West Coast technology firm, adjusting to the new job was rough. It was difficult leaving a $20 billion corporation and joining a much smaller company. Now his boss was intimating things weren't working out. The marketing director was struggling to adapt to a different corporate culture and felt totally unappreciated for his efforts. After consulting with a HeartMath trainer, he was determined to FREEZE-FRAME his concerns about his boss's attitude toward him. As he did, he realized that his severe judgments of the man were causing terrible difficulties in communication, affecting the boss's perception of his effectiveness. He also recognized that while the boss's managerial style was not up to par, the man was under pressure to reach the sales goals. The dynamics between the two men quickly improved and the marketing director was relieved. He still has the job, new excitement for his work, and a better relationship with his boss.

This marketing director had a valuable insight into his mechanical thought processes. He realized that the power to step back from a situation and gain increased perception of the hidden factors involved made all the difference. This new awareness and the release it brought also inspired him to apply Freeze-Framing at home.

Releasing Job Anxiety

Just before Christmas, an editor at a U.S. magazine had an argument with his publisher, who threatened to fire him. Anxiety consumed his holidays, affecting his wife and children. Clearly he was the one ruining his holiday. He Freeze-Framed and shifted to his heart for a new perspective. He reflected on all his skills and background, and knew that even if he lost the job, his talents were marketable. Upon his return, the relationship warmed up again and the editor was grateful he hadn't devitalized any more of his energy.

Failing to manage fear and anxiety ages the human system like miles age a car. Look at the psychological equations:

Before FREEZE-FRAME:

Communication Conflict = Fear + Tension + Anxiety = Stress

After FREEZE-FRAME:

Stress + FREEZE-FRAME = Perception Shift + Reframe + Release = Improved Communication

THE MENTAL BENEFITS

As you learn to FREEZE-FRAME, your mind will be one of the big winners. In the business examples above, the people's mental perspectives were clouding their reactions, inducing stress and ineffectiveness. What you want is fresh, clear-headed perception — the kind an ideal judge would have. Our image of a good judge in a court of law would be one who has acquired the self-control to hear with his heart, not just his head. Remember, by "heart" I don't mean emotionalism. I mean intuitive intelligence. The ideal judge would use the two working jointly in balance — head and heart — to clearly see all sides, then put together a summary of his findings. Do you think he could do this with his mind knowing solely what it knows? He would have earned his position in life by being able to suspend his opinions, so he could take in the whole picture. What about our own inner judge? How balanced can our perspectives be if we are under stress? Let's take a mental stress check.

Which of these mental stresses apply to you?

❑ Frequently judge myself for not being the way I'd like to be?

❑ Often blame or resent others if things don't go well?

❑ Feel like I don't have control over my life?

❑ Mental anguish?

❑ Worry about the future or the past?

❑ Often distracted?

❑ Can't shut my mind off and relax?

❑ Other?_____

How does FREEZE-FRAME turn these mental stress deficits into assets? As we said in Chapter Four, FREEZE-FRAME helps balance the two-way communication between the heart and brain which in turn regulates heart rate, blood pressure and nervous system. Perceptions and emotional reactions are transmitted between the physical heart and brain via the nervous system. When you FREEZE-FRAME, a different electrical signal is triggered in the higher perceptual center in the brain to bring about an intuitive and more balanced perspective of any situation. As you engage in Freeze-Framing, new solutions can reach the mind. This is significant for effective decision-making. People highly skilled in FREEZE-FRAME actually calm the brain waves each time they do it, then experience an increased flow of intuitive understanding and increased power to adapt.

The mind, of course, cannot manage itself, and often limits itself (and you) by thinking that what it already knows is all there is to know. In the information era, it's important to remain open and flexible. Data constantly bombards us, forcing society through fast-paced changes. FREEZE-FRAME allows you to take in and sort data quickly so the brain can file it in memory for use when needed. As this skill increases, your intuitive intelligence becomes more active and available, offering the mind valuable new insights it can't receive on its own. In this way, your mind can break out of the boxes it has contrived through what I call "hand-me-down" programs. These are old mindsets and thought patterns that limit perception and options. It's hard to let go of these thought patterns because they're comfortable and much of our security has been based on them. It's the lack of self-security that keeps people clinging to old "hand-me-down" mind habits that have proven to be nonefficient and noneffective. As you activate the intuition more consistently, you find a deeper security than acquired intellectual knowledge brings. Knowledge is always changing, but wisdom, through the heart-activated intuition, is deeper and wider in its scope. Wisdom gives you the power to handle changes at high speed without losing your sense of security.

Family Conflicts — Knowing What You Know

The story of Nick, Maria and Tracy was an example of a typical conflict that happens frequently between parents and teens. It's called, "Parents believe they know best and teens think they know best." Tracy couldn't understand why she couldn't drive the new car. Nick thought his daughter was out of line for even asking to borrow the car. Each "knows what they know" and wouldn't even talk to the other. An obvious and all too common problem. The consequences of "knowing what you know" and not being open to new perceptions can be seen in the stress epidemic and turmoil throughout the world. The increasing numbers of high school drop-outs, run-aways, and youthful offenders are evidence of a huge gap between parents, teens and our educational system repeatedly caused by "knowing what you know."

The largest problem, according to teenagers, is that parents (and adults in general) don't listen. Parents feel teens don't listen. If teens don't act as they are expected to, parents throw up their hands and ask, "Where did I go wrong?" It doesn't have to be this way. In our efforts with at-risk youth, the Institute facilitates workshops between adults and teens to boost communication and understanding across the generations. Following one such session in Phoenix, an eighth-grade "gang-banger," who had been involved with a gang for several years, participated in a listening exercise between himself and a woman who worked for the school district. The woman was amazed at the sensitivity of this "known trouble-maker" and felt tremendous compassion for him. After the program the boy went to the Vice Principal and, with tears in his eyes, told him this was the first time an adult had ever listened to him. As a result, he found the courage to leave the gang.

Leveraged Intelligence

If you're mentally on overload and can't shut off

your mind, you may feel you have lost mental control. And you have. You've become a victim of your own mind. To turn mental stress into an asset, FREEZE-FRAME and shift to neutral. Then listen to your heart to achieve power over mind ramblings. As you act from heart intuition, the mind can shift gears and go in a healthier direction. When you shift an attitude, energy starts to follow in that direction.

People often attempt to think positively without first making an *attitude shift* and then wonder why nothing changes. It's because attitudes contain feelings and it takes more than a few positive thoughts to re-route the feelings contained in an attitude — especially a negatively slanted attitude (like resentment, poor self-image, etc.). On its own, the mind struggles and usually fails in building attitude shifts without the strength and forbearance of the heart's commitment. Approaching attitude changes from the heart-feeling level makes it easier to secure a lasting shift.

People will achieve more of their personal goals in the future as they truly learn to "put heart into what they do." Freeze-Framing is a window of opportunity to engage your heart feelings in your decision-making. It offers you deeper understanding of issues the mind often overlooks. With practice you can shift gears and produce energy-saving attitude adjustments throughout the day. You gain what I call "leveraged intelligence" with practical applications. It's leveraged intelligence that restrains you from inviting and repeating the same stress patterns that drain your system and dilute your peace. Leveraged intelligence emerges when the mind and the heart share the same "think tank" before taking action.

Here's a common situation many people face almost daily. A teacher is in the middle of a deadline. She has a report to finish that requires focused attention. The phone rings. It's the principal. He says, "The report last week was completely wrong. It didn't cover this and you didn't do that!" He hangs up with, "And you must have this week's done by 3:00 p.m. Don't be late." Well, there goes her focus — right out the window. She becomes distracted with thoughts of how unfair he is, how many times he's bullied her in the past, how she wishes he'd do his own reports. It's difficult to continue working. After ten minutes, she realizes she's hardly written a word and concludes it's time to FREEZE-FRAME. In a minute or two she has made her way to neutral. Here is her report of what happened after that.

> "When I felt I'd evened out, I had a calm talk with myself to put things into perspective. I asked myself, 'What would be a better response to this situation?' My common sense said, 'I do work for Joe (the principal). He does pay me to do it the way he wants. Maybe there's another approach. Let's take a broader look at what I'm trying to accomplish.' I admitted that I wanted to do well on this report for the school board because it could help get money for some essential supplies. That's why Joe was concerned that it be done right. With my racing mind and angry emotions out of the way, I finished the report in record time and even had fun doing it. In the past, without FREEZE-FRAME, I would have gotten it done, somehow, but I would have depleted my energy level with stress and resentment throughout the process."
> S.N., *Nashville, TN*

Can you see the clarity and common sense here? It's *you* you want to do this for. It's not the principal's problem to finish the report on time. Whether your boss is Attila the Hun is not the issue. It's you who pays — mentally, emotionally, and physically — if you fail to respond effectively to life situations.

The choice is simple:

1. Get upset, irritated or frustrated and cloud your own mental perceptions. It will be like crawling through quicksand to get to the end of the job.

Or,

2. Do what it takes to clear the deck so that lucid thinking can come through.

Go ahead and look after yourself. It's your own wear and tear, nobody else's. It's your job and how you choose to go about it depends on you.

Studying with Clarity

When you're trying to store information, your mind can become so overloaded it ceases to function well. If you FREEZE-FRAME periodically, you can recharge mentally, emotionally and physically, while increasing memory retention and comprehension. A real estate agent was studying for an exam that would allow him to advance his career. He described how Freeze-Framing helped him retain what was critical. As he pored over reams of data, he was able to absorb information quickly with increased clarity instead of cramming till he was beat. While studying, if you practice this one-minute exercise at the start and again at those points where you begin to feel overloaded, you'll build mental assets and leveraged intelligence.

Increased Creativity

During a creative project like writing, designing a new brochure or product, gardening, carpentry, or any hobby, Freeze-Framing can expand and develop your creativity. It yields more intuitive perception at any time. You don't have to wait until you're in stress. Leveraged intelligence multiplies as you apply this technology for intuitive access to all aspects of your life.

> Creativity + FREEZE-FRAME = Intuitive access + Leveraged intelligence = Added enjoyment and quality of life

THE EMOTIONAL BENEFITS

People know their emotions can be like a dark cloud, making it difficult to see solutions. FREEZE-FRAME will help you calm your emotions so they won't keep rampaging the mind. When the emotions are backed off, your mind has a chance to achieve clear common sense. In talking about the necessity of managing the emotions, I'm not trying to imply that your emotions are the bad guy in the human system, or that FREEZE-FRAME is intended to suppress them. I am saying that you'll save energy when you learn to first neutralize their intent before you engage them. When the heat of the emotions is turned down, the mind can see more options and more solutions. As research has proven, when your unmanaged emotions fuel negative thought patterns, you pay a price in accelerated aging, weakened immune system and impaired cardiovascular function. Letting excessive negative emotion blow through your system is like having a big hole blow right through your balloon of energy. Everything can be drained out of you in a matter of moments. It can take hours, days, even weeks to recover. Some people suffer this so frequently, they never "recover." They never experience the kind of clarity that comes with emotional balance.

When the emotions are *managed*, not suppressed, they can be used to add more fun, texture and quality to life. They are like free fuel for your system; but if left unmanaged they're highly flammable. As you find balance between your heart and your head, your emotions turn into creative passion and become a tremendous asset. Creatively directing that focused passion is fun. To turn emotional deficits into rewarding assets, we first need to recognize emotional stress.

Which of these emotional stresses apply to you?

❑ Quick to get irritated, frustrated or angry?

❑ Feeling unloved or unliked?

❑ Frequent hurt feelings?

❑ Moodiness — lots of ups and downs?

❑ Depression?

❑ Afraid of losing emotional control?

❑ Fears or phobias?

❑ Other?_____

Emotional energy is really neutral. It follows and adds feeling to your thoughts and attitudes. Here's a story to illustrate. Your wife's sister, we'll call Jane, has come to visit for a few months while she gets her feet back on the ground after a divorce. Jane is one of those people who just "rubs you the wrong way." You never say a word but every time she does "that Jane thing," the irritation stacks up on top of all the other irritations. With every new layer on the stack you feel the negative emotions building like a balloon about to pop. One day, that over-loaded balloon you've been pumping reaches the breaking point. Out comes all the old stale hot air on top of poor Jane. She reacts with an array of hurt feelings. For the next week, just seeing each other feels like a close encounter between two porcupines. Not a very efficient situation to be in — all because *you* finally had to release all that built up pressure. Even though it's a release in one respect, you generate an energy leak that's hard to recoup.

Let's turn this story around and go back to the beginning when things are starting to build up and you feel that emotional energy adding amp to your feelings. FREEZE-FRAME as soon as you realize that distortion is happening. Go through the steps. Find your neutral zone and let some air out of the balloon. If you can reach a clear point and remove the excess emotional energy, you might go to your heart again for ways to talk to Jane like a friend and work out what's bothering you. You're not perfect either, but you both need to discover a way to live in the same house, even if it's only for a few months. That's a lot of time together not to be enjoying it, much less creating an energy deficit for Jane, yourself and your wife. It makes a lot more sense to find harmonious approaches to issues, even if your threshold of tolerance has been crossed. That's serious preventive maintenance.

It's your own mental, emotional and physical health you promote by reframing your attitudinal approaches to people and issues in life. But these kinds of thoughts will never have a chance if you don't pull back and calm those emotions.

Emotional outbursts are tricky. Here's why. How many times have you heard someone say, "It felt good to get angry and tell that S.O.B. off." It *can* feel good, in the moment, to get your emotions out. Getting them out is usually better than holding them in. The problem is that emotional outbursts often come with a price tag of additional stress and another mess to clean up later. Oftentimes the person you've dumped on doesn't remember your *message*, they just remember the *onslaught*. So you haven't really solved the problem, probably just added to it. As you learn to FREEZE-FRAME those highly charged emotions, you also learn to communicate directly to people without all the extra voltage that can cause them to be defensive, while frying your nerves and draining your energy bank.

Here's an illustration. The owner of an East Coast company was telling a group of employees about a new product the company was planning to launch. The announcement was greeted with immense enthusiasm from everyone, except one man who had a history of resisting new ideas. The man informed the owner that not only did he think the new product was *not* a good idea for the company, he would do everything possible to forestall its reaching the market. The owner's immediate reaction was anger, but as he Freeze-Framed, he remembered the man was actually a very effective individual whom numerous customers raved about. Instead of continuing to react with anger as he normally would have done, the boss listened and decided to appreciate the qualities of the employee that made him so effective. Their discussion continued in an open, frank manner. The employee, surprised the boss didn't react with his usual high-pitched anger, began to see the benefits of the product, and the boss saw some new perspectives. The product still came out, but slightly modified, based on the suggestions of the employee.

Fear

People live in fear. Fear of rejection, fear of being hurt, fear of the future, fear of speaking in public — the list of phobias is long. While it is not my intention in this book to address the emotion of fear in great detail, I would like to say that many fears can be lessened by Freeze-Framing. The technique gives you a chance to engage the power of your heart to calm fear reactions and gain more objectivity. Take the fear of speaking in public. Freeze-Framing can comfort you into neutral, relaxing the knot in your stomach or the quiver in your voice, so you're no longer paralyzed by your fear. With practice, the technique will activate positive feelings and perspectives that can actually release the fear. Here's a dramatic example of FREEZE-FRAME's effectiveness from the former assistant police chief of San Jose, California.

> "During my 30-year career, I've been required to make many speeches and I also taught at the college level for seven years. I developed an ability to speak in front of a classroom of fifty without any problem. When I became Assistant Chief I was asked to speak in front of a packed convention hall of 500 police officers and their families

for a promotional ceremony. It was really a shock when I walked in there. I was well prepared because preparation is supposed to reduce anxiety, but I got tremendously anxious. I became very warm and started to perspire. I said to myself, 'This is not me.' I'm normally under control so much better than that. I have negotiated hostage situations but at that moment I would rather have been negotiating a hostage release than making that speech. So I Freeze-Framed and an unbelievable calm came over me just before I had to begin. I spoke from the heart and really didn't look over my notes. It went over beautifully. Afterwards, I received several comments from people who said it had been the best speech they had ever heard during a promotional ceremony. One woman even came up to me saying it was the first time she had wanted to cry at one of these ceremonies." *B.M., San Jose, CA*

Depression

Depression is an emotional distress call suffered by millions. Let me share with you the report of a woman who used Freeze-Framing to overcome her chronic depression. She had been seeing a psychiatrist, taking lithium for over a year, but wasn't improving. Her husband and two young children were distraught that they were unable to help. After reading our book *The Hidden Power of the Heart,* she attended a Heart Empowerment training and had a private consultation with a HeartMath trainer. The trainer noticed the woman was constantly voicing how terrible a person she was, invariably putting herself down. She asked the woman to practice

Freeze-Framing and appreciate something in her life every time she noticed she was putting herself down. The woman sincerely practiced for two days. During that time, she felt her heart open and could sense happiness again. As she continued to practice, her perceptions began to change and her mind started to show her new possibilities. It was as if the sun was coming out after a long dark, cloudy winter. One month later, her therapist confirmed the change was real and she was able to stop taking drugs.

People live for the moments when their hearts come alive. That doesn't just mean on Valentine's Day. FREEZE-FRAME is especially designed to help you activate positive feelings in your heart *at will*. Many people feel so unloved or unliked they find it hard to feel love, especially for themselves. Millions suffer from mood swings, feeling great one minute and terrible the next. Mood altering drugs are in great demand because people simply want to feel better more of the time. Your most productive drugs are within your own endocrine system. You feel alive and have additional energy and vitality — depending on your hormonal flow. You influence this flow more than you know by how much you manage your mental and emotional perceptions and reactions. You are your own self-pharmacist, more so than you would think. Learning to put your emotions in neutral helps you access the inner prescription that accomplishes the best overall health.

THE PHYSICAL BENEFITS

Usually people are aware of obvious physical stresses, like aches, pains and symptoms of illness. What we're not so aware of is how accumulating inner stress can lead to serious problems later on, like high blood pressure, degenerative diseases of the immune system, accelerated aging, or heart problems.

Which of these physical stresses apply to you?

❑ Frequent aches or pains?

❑ Too many colds, congestion or respiratory ailments?

❑ Frequent fatigue or feeling run down?

❑ Chronic or major illness?

❑ Accident prone?

❑ Other? _____

We all would love to find the fountain of youth. But to come upon a big waterfall labeled "Drink here; you've found it!" might not happen. Let's take a subtler look at what youth really means on the inside. Everyone knows how refreshing a child's energy can be. Children have a certain liquid flexibility that "goes with the flow." They play with all their hearts and if they fall down and scrape their knee, once the Band-Aid is on, they're usually back into the swing of things fast. To find an adult with these same qualities is not so easy. What happened to us? Where did it go? Did our spirits age too? That's what a fountain would be good for — to fill us back up with childlike qualities of enthusiasm, flexibility and the zest for adventure no matter how difficult our life experience has been.

I'm not saying FREEZE-FRAME is intended to be the fountain of youth, a new religion or new philosophy.

People have to work out their own beliefs about life within themselves. However this tool can often "save your tail" while you try to work all that out for yourself. It's a simple, scientific approach to your own health and well-being. Don't let the simplicity throw you. Because Freeze-Framing is so simple, we went through painstaking experiments in the lab to prove or disprove its effectiveness. It's the very simplicity of FREEZE-FRAME that's creating all the testimonies of excitement. Something that's simple and works? The laboratory proof says yes.

Slowing the Aging Process

To age mentally and emotionally denotes a loss of flexibility and a loss of the ability to adapt. You become a person who doesn't like to do anything you don't usually do — and nobody can change your mind. You are just *like* that, 'set in stone.' Doesn't that sound like age, becoming set in your ways? You've lost the childlike feeling that life's an adventure, with new events to experience and enjoy. Aging is a part of life. But to age naturally, with a childlike heart, can keep the sparkle, spontaneity, and adventure in your life.

Remember, FREEZE-FRAME is a one-minute technique. It's like a Swiss Army knife — a convenient tool to use anywhere. What if you have an opportunity to go on a camping trip with friends, but have to give up your usual routine for a few days in order to get ready? After all, there are bags to pack, supplies to gather, plants to water, pets to feed. What a hassle! The further you explore it, it's really too much trouble. It just wouldn't be worth it.

Do you feel *age* setting in? From a scientific perspective, aging happens when our cells lose flexibility and the ability to adapt. We become crystallized in certain habits and attitudes that are harder and harder to change. But it's being proven in the lab that the positive hormones you create within your own system with positive feelings do more for your regeneration than you might know.

If you are unable to make a flexible decision, FREEZE-FRAME. Shift your thoughts away from knowing what you know about yourself. Focus your attention in your heart and go to neutral. Hold that for a moment or two. Then ask yourself — without the "I don't want to's" interfering — what would be the most rewarding thing to do? Recall what it feels like to be with friends, laughing, having fun, and going on adventures. If that camping trip still doesn't feel right for you (sometimes it won't), you have at least given it a fair shot. Then you can make your decision and feel right about it. Take that moment and find clarity on what you *really* want to do, beneath the usual mind resistances and thoughts like "It's just not *convenient.*" This way, after the car pulls out and the friends are off to play, you won't have any second thoughts or regret your choice. So much stress is created by people wishing they'd made different decisions in life. Learn to make peace with life as it is, then you develop more power to change it for the better.

Reducing Physical Symptoms

As you build your sense of personal power through Freeze-Framing, you are likely to find physical benefits as well. Essi Systems, the stress research firm mentioned in Chapter One, has found a direct link between back pain and the lack of personal power. Each time you FREEZE-FRAME, you are building personal power and recharging your batteries. It's quite amazing how much healing and regenerative power the human system has when body, mind and emotions are in sync rather than fighting each other. The next time you feel run down or have an annoying ache or pain, try Freeze-Framing. (This is not instead of taking medication that might be appropriate, but as an add-on.) Let the body shut down for a few moments while you calm the mind and emotions. Frequently, the annoyance we feel when the physical body is hurting or sick only adds to the discomfort and lengthens the healing process.

In our AIDS research study mentioned in Chapter Four, most participants reported a significant reduction in opportunistic infections following their practice of FREEZE-FRAME and other HeartMath tools. Of the individuals who reported frequent physical symptoms at the start of the study (such as diarrhea, nausea, loss of weight, rashes, fevers, flu symptoms), 44% reported no negative physical symptoms by the end of the study.*

Saving Money while Improving Employee Health

Due to rising health care costs, IHM and three small companies decided to self-insure their entire staff and their families. In exchange for the staff's agreement to practice FREEZE-FRAME and other HeartMath self-management techniques, the companies paid all health care costs — medical, dental, prescription drugs, chiropractic, preventive health care, and all deductibles — and provided free FREEZE-FRAME training for the staff and their families. In the first three years of the program, 1991-1993,

---

*This study was appropriately named AIDS FOR HOPE, providing participants with tools as in 'aids' to achieve less stressful and more 'hopeful' lives.

health care costs averaged an amazing $350 per person per year, less than one-tenth the national average.*

THE SPORTS BENEFITS

Playing sports can be one of your most fun and re-generating activities, but sports is also a major source of stress for many. A 1994 survey of golfers in Japan revealed that pressure to perform well at golf is causing an alarming number of heart attacks. Most people who enjoy sports want to improve their health — not lose it — while they sharpen their game.

If you're a sports enthusiast you may have lofty expectations of your own performance. Competition can breed tremendous pressure, especially if self-image, money or a prize is involved. People react to this pressure by getting tense at exactly the time they need mental and physical flexibility. The outcome can be mental and physical under-performance known as "choking in the clutch." Great players have the ability to stay loose and make the great play. FREEZE-FRAME technology has been proven to help people stay loose under pressure while enhancing their passion for achievement.

Increasingly, people are waking up to the importance of getting their mind and emotions entrained for sustained success. Entrainment, as I explained in Chapter Four, occurs when your heart rhythms are harmonious, your parasympathetic and sympathetic nervous systems are in balance, and your mind and emotions feel in sync. All systems are in tune. The number one ranked

---

*Editor's note: This information does not imply that using the FREEZE-FRAME technology will create these results in all situations or that companies should abandon their health care plans.

tennis player in 1994, Pete Sampras, has become famous for his focused, even-keeled nature during competition. He doesn't get overly excited when he makes a great shot nor overly disturbed when he blows a shot. He has a sense of humor that helps him stay balanced without suppressing his emotions. Recently, one of the world's top ranked players of the '80s and winner of several Grand Slams stated that if he had managed his emotions better during his career, he would have won more matches. The FREEZE-FRAME technique is an excellent way to increase your leverage in any sport without sacrificing your fun or your health. Here is just one of many stories to illustrate.

Finding the Groove

"Golf is more than a game to me — it's a passion. I tend to be disgusted after a poor shot, then lose my ability to focus on the next one. I tried various methods to improve my concentration but found they didn't succeed. When I was taught the FREEZE-FRAME technique, I immediately recognized its potential to improve concentration and attunement to the target, the ball and my swing. The very next day I was scheduled to play golf with my boss and some prestigious clients, so I decided to put FREEZE-FRAME to the test. I practiced Freeze-Framing after each stroke or putt, good or bad. To my amazement, my rhythm and timing as well as my concentration drastically improved. The mechanics of my swing had fallen naturally into 'the groove.' I shot my all-time best round and have been using the FREEZE-FRAME technique with great success in my golf

game ever since. I also utilize it in the office when clear focus and self-control are demanded."
W.K., Menlo Park, CA

People who watch sports also experience stress. Some get so over-identified when their team loses, they remain upset for days and manufacture stress-producing hormones the whole time. Using FREEZE-FRAME presents a chance for the heart to tell the mind to release and let go because a lost game is not going to undo itself. Repetitive over-identity with losing induces stress on the heart and immune system, often resulting in physical ailments. People don't know what caused their ailments, especially if they were in good physical shape from a balanced diet and exercise program. Patterns of mental and emotional chaos can play a major role in strangling the physical body's vitality, aging it before its time. People then take prescription drugs to assist the physical body, but time and again these drugs create complications in mental and emotional areas which were often the source of the problems in the first place. The no-win merry-go-round!

Freeze-Framing isn't intended to take the fun, excitement and drama out of watching or playing sports. It's designed to help you remember "it's only a game," so if the outcome isn't to your liking, you won't take it out on your family, co-workers, or your immune system.

Chapter Six

Social Benefits and Applications

U p to this point we've focused mainly on how you
will benefit mentally, emotionally, physically, in
business, and in sports as you learn to use FREEZE-FRAME.
Now let me to talk about the benefits for intimate relationships and for society at large.

THE RELATIONSHIP BENEFITS

Relationship issues can form a massive merry-go-
round of overcare and stress, causing a steady drain in
your system, affecting your work, health, and entire well-
being. You can feel lonely without a relationship and in
conflict when you're in one. How do you win? FREEZE-
FRAME helps you access balance and power within yourself so you can approach relationship issues more effectively.

Social Benefits and Applications

Which of these relationship stresses apply to you?

❏ Loneliness?

❏ Jealousy of others?

❏ Insecure?

❏ Relationship doesn't meet my expectations?

❏ Sexual frustration?

❏ Separation or divorce issues?

❏ Other?_____

Sexual frustration, jealousy, envy, fear of rejection and loneliness are all major energy leaks that sap personal power and vitality. Many people don't think of these insecure feelings as stress but they can have serious health consequences and take an enormous toll on our well-being. Whether you are single, married or divorced, relationship issues can become so sticky or problematic, some leveraged intelligence is required. According to *The Language of the Heart*, by Dr. James Lynch,

> "Medical statistics on the loss of human companionship, the lack of love, and human loneliness quickly revealed that the expression *broken heart* is not just a poetic image for loneliness and despair but is an overwhelming medical reality. All the available data pointed to the lack of human companionship, chronic loneliness, social isolation or the sudden loss of a loved one as being among the leading causes of premature death in the U.S.A. And while we found that the effects of human loneliness were related to virtually every

major disease — whether cancer, pneumonia or mental disease — they were particularly apparent in heart disease, the leading cause of death in the U.S.A. Evidently millions of people were dying, quite literally, of broken hearts... At practically every age, for both sexes and all races, death rates for the single, the widowed, and the divorced [or unhappily married], range anywhere from two to ten times higher than for married individuals... Many heart patients seem strangely oblivious to their own loneliness, disconnected from any real awareness of their emotional pain."*

Not only do relationship problems cause enormous stress, mentally and emotionally, this research reveals that the physical heart can pay a serious price as well. As health care costs increase, relationship stress becomes not just a personal issue but a societal concern. Relationship loss can be one of the most traumatic human experiences. Some people never recover. One of the biggest challenges in a relationship break-up occurs when one person wants to move on and the other clings to the relationship. If you're the one clinging, it can feel like the world is caving in and all hope for fulfillment is lost. Your entire self feels like life has turned against you; there is an empty place inside that no one can fill except the one who doesn't seem to care anymore. You've become a victim of your own dependence on another person's "batteries." How could something as simple as FREEZE-FRAME help?

If you're stuck mentally and emotionally in relationship stress, FREEZE-FRAME can present a fresh perspective and intuitive direction. If there were ever a time to turn to your heart power for help, it's now. The paradox

---

*The Language of the Heart, James J. Lynch, Ph.D., Basic Books

is that it seems like your heart is broken, so how could it mend itself? And at those times, if you attempt to go to your heart you just feel pain. What do you do?

There is hope. Research is showing that while the physical heart is indeed taxed when you feel your heart has been broken, the road to recovery does not have to be long and arduous. A broken heart starts with broken mental and emotional attachments and expectations. Feelings of rejection, hurt and disappointment have gotten mixed in with the real love you felt. The mind replays the hurt over and over, magnifying the pain so it feels like your heart is broken and all love is lost. FREEZE-FRAME can help you extract the real love from the hurt and pain and re-open your heart. With use you can reclaim your own power and gain new hope for the future. Here's a classic example of a broken relationship and how practicing FREEZE-FRAME helped the healing process.

"I came home from a weekend away and asked my boyfriend how his weekend was. He declared he had been looking for his own apartment! I was shocked and went into immediate despair. Everything went black and all I could feel was numbness and pain. My emotional panic and insecurity were so strong I didn't know how to deal with them. We'd been living together for a year and although we had a few recent arguments, they were nothing that I thought couldn't be fixed. I had no idea he would leave. For the first two weeks, I couldn't function at home or at work. I alternated between feeling miserable, feeling I'd never be loved again, and being angry. I cried all the time. I'd come home at night and cry myself to sleep. I knew I couldn't go on like this. I had to do something, so I decided to practice the FREEZE-FRAME tool I'd learned. At first the pain was so strong, all I could do was become neutral. If I tried to feel love, it would just trigger the hurt and pain with renewed fervor. It surprised me that in reaching neutral, I began to feel better. Although I still couldn't discover anything to appreciate about what had happened, I decided to sincerely practice appreciating other things in my life. The emotional roller coaster ride stopped and I started to gain a new sense of peace. I began to feel better about myself as a person which also surprised me. It required about a month of practicing going to neutral before I could start forgiving him and moving on. But it worked.

"Now it's six months later and we're actually great friends and getting along better than we ever had. There's no romantic involvement, but we have regained the close friendship and the feeling of love, while letting go of the attachment and expectations of a relationship. The last time I had a rough break-up, when my fiancé left me, it took nine months of pain to get over it. I thought it was impossible to regain friendship after an intimate relationship ended. With FREEZE-FRAME, I have been able to release the hurt and re-open communication. "

Many people retreat into loneliness after a relationship loss closes their heart. Re-opening the heart is essential to the recovery process. Freeze-Framing can speed up that recovery time and help open the next chapter of your life.

A psychologist who found success using the FREEZE-FRAME tool in her own life, began to teach it to her clients. One couple she was counseling had years of built-up resentments about each other they couldn't shake. If ever a marriage was on the rocks, theirs was. The psychologist asked them to practice the FREEZE-FRAME technique each time thoughts or feelings of hurt, resentment or blame came up. If one started to argue, they were both to call a FREEZE-FRAME time-out, access their heart intuition for direction and listen to it. The results were clinically amazing to the therapist. For the first few days Freeze-Framing defused the emotional arguing. They both would become very quiet as they practiced. This caused a veil to lift, revealing new understanding. Each perceived clearly how their own private process of blaming the other for every new incident of non-caring or non-communication would drag up memories of previous times. Before they knew it they'd be in a full-scale war. Each argument had been enflamed by these internal agendas. Upon Freeze-Framing, their intuitions offered them surprising new options. Their relationship began to improve. At the following therapy session, each described to the psychologist how they were the one, not the *other*, perpetuating the ongoing war. They cut out the blame and changed their own reactions instead of trying to change the other. After a few weeks they began re-experiencing moments of the love and appreciation they felt when they first were married.

When people drift away from each other in a relationship, it's hard to re-bridge the gap without first bridging the gap between one's own heart and mind. By attempting that, new hope is often born.

In today's lifestyle, people don't have time for long

drawn-out therapy. Things are moving too fast and most can't afford it anyhow. Many relationship break-ups could be spared if people deepened the connection between their own hearts and minds. Freeze-Framing helps each partner make that inner connection within themselves first, then with each other. Shallow, veneer communication creates most of the stress deficit in individuals, relationships, businesses, communities and society. People have to earn their way out. Learning to manage the mind and emotions is a profitable place to start. Using FREEZE-FRAME hands you a convenient mirror for self-review.

THE SOCIAL BENEFITS

Which of these social stresses apply to you?

❏ Financial pressures?

❏ Have everything but bored with life?

❏ Not enough time for family, friends, or hobbies?

❏ Concerns about child-rearing and family values?

❏ Fear of crime, violence, or disasters?

❏ Other? _____

Financial pressures have become so commonplace, they often create constant anxiety affecting all aspects of life. Anxiety makes it difficult to perceive creative solutions. Anxiety can also warp your perspective so you project that you will only be happy if you have more money, more gadgets, a better house, car, job, etc. Financial pressures can be quite real when bills are due, especially if one member of the household has lost a job or you're trying to send your kids to college. These money pressures affect so many diverse things, the *time* you have for family and friends, the *attitudes* you hold in raising your children, etc. The Freeze-Framing technique assists your heart in understanding what *your* core values really are — what you and your family really require for balance and fulfillment — and managing your emotions in the now. FREEZE-FRAME is not a magic wand that will pay your bills or provide two months' vacation every year. But it can help you become mentally and emotionally managed while dealing with your current challenges — and remember to do what you may already know deep inside.

Here's the social reality today: No matter how hard we try to prevent it, life will still throw us curve balls just when we're not prepared. Major changes can happen so fast. One minute you're fine and the next can be a mess, or somewhere in between. One minute your job is secure, the next minute the company is laying off 15%. One moment you're asleep, the next moment you're picking through the rubble from the earthquake, tornado, flood, fire, or hurricane that just rolled through town. Life is going to be life. That's why it's important to establish your values and priorities now. The FREEZE-FRAME technology is designed to assist you in discovering what your values really are and help you *remember* to live them when the pressure starts to throw you off-kilter. Practicing releases pressure before it accumulates.

How about a backyard story of how even simple social interactions can start out fun, then quickly turn into a mess to clean up later? You're at your next door neighbor Sam's house for a barbecue. It's been a rough week and you're counting on having some fun. You arrive, and before you know it, you've offended Sam. Tension increases. Sam goes a little overboard with his reaction. After all, you were merely joking about his yard never being mowed, "Cows would love to be invited to lunch someday!" You thought you were being funny but nobody laughed. Well, here is a perfect place to grab FREEZE-FRAME. If you acknowledge what could happen next, and step back quickly, you might be able to prevent a mess caused by your *faux pas*. If not, once he lashes out about your old car giving a cheap look to the other driveways in the neighborhood and you respond with anger — well there goes the party. Not only have you messed up a fun time for yourself but you've probably dumped a very wet blanket on everyone else, too. Through remembering the technique, you can frame that split second bail-out, preventing much conflict and stress. By chilling out, you can work it out and often avoid the worst case scenarios. Managed reactions save days' of energy.

Inner Violence — The Rage Within Us

Realize that much domestic violence usually starts off with a few angry words and a few hurt feelings that don't get resolved, then escalates into feelings of betrayal, rage, and revenge. Inner feelings of rage soon spill over into all aspects of society. Social stress multiplies daily with every new report of a drive-by shooting, rape, child abuse, children bringing guns to school, homelessness, ethnic violence or some other crisis. The root cause of a lot of these social stresses is the inner violence created by dysfunctional communication between the heart and the mind. As social stress increases, we're faced with a choice: Retreat into fear and isolation, become angry and bitter, try to ignore it all, or take responsibility for our own stress reactions. *It's how we as individuals handle our seemingly innocent daily stresses that determines our ability to weather the bigger storms.*

Social disasters happen every day, often hidden from the public eye. The Institute of HeartMath provides FREEZE-FRAME training to people who work on the front lines of the social battlefield. Here's one of our many experiences.

"Tom and Sheila always wished they could be foster parents, to share the love they felt in their marriage with children who needed a family. A case worker offered them three young boys who had witnessed their parents commit a murder/suicide. The boys had already been through three foster homes. The eldest, age 9, was especially hostile, angry and virtually impossible to reach. With grave reservation, Tom and Sheila took on the situation, but after a week were deeply concerned they had made a tragic mistake. While on a break from a seminar I was giving for church and community leaders in Atlanta, I met Tom and Sheila. Their oldest boy was acting wild and impossible to control. I took ten minutes to teach the parents how to FREEZE-FRAME.

"One week later, they told their minister they were discovering a new sense of family by keeping their own balance through the use of FREEZE-FRAME. I saw them two months later and they looked like a normal family, having a picnic on a lawn. The boys were energetic, excited, and playful and responded to their new parents as real parents. It was clear in the expressions on all their faces that something deeply transformative had occurred. Tom and Sheila couldn't speak highly enough about how FREEZE-FRAME had helped them. They added that their social worker could not believe the change in the boys either. Previously, they'd confided to the social worker that they didn't believe they could handle the situation and to look for alternative placements."

The most acute social priority is for individuals to clean up their own mental and emotional messes. As people learn *how* to be responsible for their mental and emotional disarray, new solutions can emerge which will help clean up the social chaos. This can create a foundation for sustaining social change. Unfortunately, whatever most of us have learned about mental and emotional balance, we probably did not learn in school. Rarely does our educational system address the critical issue of mental and emotional self-management. Yet it's a missing link to individual and social peace.

Further Strains on the Social Fabric

The seeming increase in natural disasters puts additional strain on our already weakened social fabric. Living through the Los Angeles earthquake of 1994 would challenge anyone's ability to cope. Here's how one person handled the disaster.

"I don't remember waking up and thinking 'we're having an earthquake.' I've lived in Southern California all my life and normally in an earthquake I will remain where I am, assessing whether or not it's a big enough quake to warrant moving to a door jamb. My first recollection of early Monday morning is being *en route* to a doorway. I'd never experienced anything quite like it. The noise, the shaking, the darkness. However, I was quite calm through the event and the early aftermath. After the quake ended, we checked for gas leaks and got back into bed, not to sleep but to keep warm and away from broken glass. There were only two ways to spend the hour and a half until daybreak. I could think about it all — the fear, the damage, the economic consequences — or I could choose my heart. My heart seemed the efficient choice. So, I pulled the energy to my heart by Freeze-Framing, then locked into feelings of compassion and appreciation. Appreciation for my safety and compassion for my friends and for the city. With every aftershock and adrenaline rush, I repeated the process. By daybreak I was ready to begin dealing with broken glass, overturned furniture, terrorized pets. For the first few days after the quake, we had several friends without heat or electricity who stayed with us. Caring for each other, reminding each other to FREEZE-FRAME and go back to the heart, helped our nerves stay calm and carried us through.

"Less than a week after the quake, deep inside me, it felt as if the earthquake had also shaken loose old fears, hurts, judgments, and insecurities. All those ancient, bad feelings were in my face again, as if I'd let my defenses down and they'd snuck in the back door. Again I was rattled, and again the most comfortable solution was to FREEZE-FRAME and retreat to my heart for secu-

rity. The inner rattling was, for me, as big a jolt as the earthquake. It took a good 36 hours of talking, of being vulnerable, and of remembering to use the technique, but it was time and energy well spent. Not only have I regained my balance, but I have an added sense of personal empowerment and new solutions. I can also appreciate the new sense of community in the city. The feeling of family we all felt in the aftermath may not last for everyone, but I know some of us will no longer see separation in our neighborhoods. We'll choose to see unity instead."
D.R., Los Angeles

A major disaster can be like a giant forced FREEZE-FRAME: We are required to instantly change our perspective about life to deal with the unplanned crisis. The more you use your heart for security during a disaster, the quicker your nervous system and immune system adapt to the trauma experienced. It's amazing how often people report closer relationships, more sense of family and community, and the breaking down of social barriers after a catastrophe. It's as though disasters and tragedies force us to disengage from mindsets and social programming so we can take care of people. One month after the earthquake, the overall crime rate in Los Angeles was still a fraction of what it had been prior to the quake.

The Information Superhighway

One of the most exciting topics in business, government, and society today is the new information superhighway. Billions are now being spent on its design and implementation. Futurists envision every home, business, government and institution linked via a vast global information network hooked into everyone's TV or computer. Deep concerns have also been raised. What kinds of mischief will computer hackers create? Will there be the equivalent of carjackings on this highway? What about mis-information? Brainwashing? Invasion of privacy? From my point of view, there are two kinds of information highway to be built. One is in "the sky," constructed with fiber optics, high-speed digital networks and satellite up-links. The other and more important one is in "the street" — in the hearts of people. The latter has to do with the quality of information exchanged between people.

Technology obviously creates many conveniences, but it can also create more complications and complexities for people to keep up with and understand. Stress can be a big problem on the information superhighway — the stress of confused communication, questionable regulation, and possibly new forms of technological violence. FREEZE-FRAME is a technology for people to become self-engineers on the *inner information highway* first, the one between an individual's own heart and mind. This highway is a two-way communication system between the heart and the higher perceptual centers of the brain. It is the primary information highway that hasn't been built yet. The global stress deficit is the consequence of that.

Many people today are excited about building networks, but wish they had extra "beef" (more live information that could really help people) to distribute through a network. Building the inner network first will lead to genuine communication between people. This is what can create more coherent, quality communication between businesses, governments and institutions. The completed individual highway of self-communication will help restore basic peace. Then what goes across the new superhighway can be *living information*, allowing humanity to realize the full potential of technology.

Yes, FREEZE-FRAME takes you straight to the heart of the matter — that seat of common sense and clarity. Practice leads to more quality of life and freedom. The heart is the key. Living and perceiving only through the head is why life gets so confusing, stressful, and dry. Without enough heart, you feel like you're living just to survive. Through the heart you access more of your real spirit and learn to become who you really are. To stay more connected with your heart's intuition would be like a dream come true. Dreams don't have to be pie in the sky. When "sky" comes down to earth and into the street, and as the qualities of spirit are measured in the lab, the solutions to some of our major social stresses may not be so far away. Freeze-Framing aids you in becoming more sensitive to your heart's directive — the power to really change from the inside out.

So take this part to heart, and when you're having one of those talks with yourself, listen deeply to your common sense thoughts, then act on them and feel the difference. Practice this even a little bit and you'll surprise yourself with what you can accomplish. Whether it's at a party, looking after a friend, or a business deal, qualities of love, care, appreciation and especially sensitivity are a breath of fresh air. People are always drawn to anyone with those sincere qualities. They can usually lift the spirits of those around them.

Some are born with a measure of it, some of us need to practice a little more to uncover those qualities. But don't fear; since you have a heart those qualities are in you. They could just be covered up and need some help getting out. FREEZE-FRAME can, step by step, in any moment in life, help you slow down enough to check in with what your real heart and spirit would do. There is much freedom and stress prevention in learning to be your real self.

Chapter Seven

Tips on Using FREEZE-FRAME

When you start learning any new skill, there are potential pitfalls. Discouragement. Not having the time to practice. Forgetting. Whether you're a business person, truck driver, teacher, parent, or student, it's easy to get entangled in the daily routine of life. Having to remember to do something different requires sincere self-initiated efforts. As you've read, the potential benefits of Freeze-Framing for improved health, vitality and well-being are numerous. That's motivation number one. It's *you* taking care of *you*. Once you start to practice, it gets smoother, as with any skill. Before long, your common sense will help you remember.

As you feel better and see your intuition become more accessible through Freeze-Framing, you'll be propelled to continue using this tool. That's motivation number two. Freeze-Framing is *very different* from "Stop and take a deep breath" or "Stop and count to 10." Here's why. Count to 10 can be just the mind counting, which may not expand perception at all. That's why the intent of Freeze-Framing is to bring your energies to your heart. As the lab research in Chapter 4 described, activating the power of the heart provides physiological benefits along with mental and emotional clarity. The step-by-step FREEZE-FRAME technique leads you to positive feelings that empower intuitive perception. Each FREEZE-FRAME step is important: to neutralize stress, activate the power of the heart, and achieve new insight.

The best way to begin to practice FREEZE-FRAME is with those little things that come up — traffic jams, things that bug you, problems at work, etc. Some people forget to exercise their FREEZE-FRAME muscle until there's a major crisis. Since they haven't built their inner strength on smaller problems, they become discouraged when the technique doesn't immediately solve a "big one." Start small, one step at a time. You don't have to shy away from using FREEZE-FRAME on the big stressors; just remember you're building an inner muscle. Practicing on small irritations, frustrations and disappointments as they happen will give you the encouragement to FREEZE-FRAME when weightier problems arise.

You won't have to FREEZE-FRAME all your life. The whole purpose and design of this one-minute technique is to take you into an automatic process. Then it's just you managing your energies the way people are naturally capable of anyhow. Regular practice of the technique is valuable because it facilitates the process of remembering until it's automatic. Then you will be able to activate the power inherent within you with continuity.

So let me cover a few of the pitfalls that can short-circuit people's initial attempts to build their inner power.

Pitfall #1 — "I Don't Have Time for This"

Let's say you're a very busy single parent. You have the usual pressures at work, compounded by the daily juggling act of your kids' after-school activities, managing the household, errands to run, bills to pay, meals to make, clothes to wash. The list seems endless.

One morning you wake up late; finding yourself late would be your first chance to exercise your FREEZE-FRAME muscle that day. But you say, "Being late for work is a real problem. I *need* to get upset over that. I could lose my job, my kids will starve," etc., etc. There you go, justified in allowing the mind and emotions to have control over you. But you say again, "I ... really ... am ... *late!* I don't have time to FREEZE-FRAME. I need to go fast and don't have time to stop." So you race around to get ready, your mind churning over all the things that could go wrong if you show up late again. Here's your chance to take a deeper look *now* — inside yourself. Getting upset, irritated and frustrated over being late will not change the outcome, except perhaps to make it worse. But grabbing a moment to FREEZE-FRAME and realizing that you've got to handle this — one way or another — might provide you with the extra edge to collect yourself and move in a more efficient manner without the stressful repercussions. If you don't, you're liable to race out of the house forgetting your files for that important business meeting. Now you're really in trouble because the client will see you as scattered and unprepared. So there you are, at your desk, frustrated and judging yourself for being so stupid. If you had stopped *for one minute* and Freeze-Framed, you would have gained enough inner balance to step back and make sure you had everything you needed before you left the house. You would have arrived a little later, but you would have been prepared — and saved yourself from draining your mental and emotional accumulators.

You *save* time and energy when you FREEZE-FRAME. Slow down, step back a moment, put things in perspective, then move on with more efficiency. You *can* adapt and control how you respond. Managing your energy is not a foreign idea or unrealistic possibility. It's accessible.

Pitfall #2 — "But the Other Person's Not Changing"

Here's a circumstance to watch for when you're in a difficult conversation. If you are staying neutral but the other person keeps right on hammering his or her point with no regard to how fair you're playing, it could be tempting to lose your cool. Don't expect life to transform around you every time you FREEZE-FRAME. So be prepared. On the other hand, don't ignore how much your balanced attitude *can* affect the people and situations you face. Appreciate yourself for the efforts you make, regardless of the outcome. If you maintain inner balance in any given situation, whatever others do, then you are properly taking care of your own self. That's okay to do, and an intelligent choice.

Pitfall #3 — "It's Not Working"

When you're first beginning to build up strength and confidence in a new skill, the least line of resistance has a strong tendency to win out. In other words, the inclination could be to revert back to old habits of reacting or judging. And, as you encounter them, you will become more aware of just how ingrained some of the habits seem to be. You could find yourself saying, "This FREEZE-FRAME is not working." But don't despair. Remember, you used to have the same habits but were mostly *unconscious* of them and saw no alternative. Now you are *conscious* of them and have a powerful new tool to assist. Once you genuinely build strength by your own practice, it's yours — an acquired skill that can be relied on and developed more and more. It's the power to have *choice* in how you want to mentally and emotionally react to life's situations, which is a gigantic leap forward in dissolving your own stress deficit. Freeze-Framing gives you access to the valve that plugs energy leaks.

Stress Prevention — Recharging your Batteries Before They Run Down

Begin building your FREEZE-FRAME muscle *before* stress comes up. You do this by simply *Freeze-Framing and finding something or someone to appreciate several times a day, though you may feel you don't need to.* When you can FREEZE-FRAME at any time, laboratory research demonstrates the benefits in harmonious heart rhythms and increased immune response. Each moment you practice shifting your perceptions, even for only 15 or 30 seconds, it's like plugging yourself into your own battery charger. Write "Practice FREEZE-FRAME" on your daily "to do" lists or in your daily planner to remind yourself to flex that muscle. Post a note on your mirror or calendar or whatever works for you. Then, when you are really stressed about something, it will be easier to quickly FREEZE-FRAME, shift perspective, and gain more clarity because you'll be in the habit of doing it. Here's a suggestion from one of the staff at the Institute:

"We use FREEZE-FRAME in our office. All the computers are programmed with a simple signal that goes off every hour on the hour which we use as a reminder. Some people have their computer screen-saver programmed to flash 'FREEZE-FRAME.' This is a reminder to FREEZE-FRAME for a few moments — whatever is going on. If others you work with are also familiar with the technique, you can just say out loud: 'FREEZE-FRAME.' It's like a code. Just speaking the words helps people see that there may be a need for mental and emotional management in that moment. Saying the words in a loving way, without an edge of judgment or sarcasm, can often give the other person a chance to stop and self-adjust in the moment — or at least recognize that their energy may be out of balance. Using 'FREEZE-FRAME' as a code has helped speed up the adjustment process in myself and others in a fun way." *E.C., Director, Military Programs, IHM*

Write It Down

When practicing FREEZE-FRAME, it's sometimes helpful to write down the issue, your typical mental and emotional reaction, and the answer your intuition gives you. But there are different ways for different people. I understand some people aren't natured to write a lot down. I'm not. But for the ones who are, you may find this helpful.

Creating a Support System

Using FREEZE-FRAME in a family, school or work environment is particularly effective when several people are practicing it. It assists each person in seeing what would be impulsive reactions and judgments, then presents them with a chance to take more responsible action. The result is individuals learning to be responsible for their own energies and decisions, people who clean up their mental messes before they even make them. As people utilize this tool together in business, school or family situations, it helps clean up the psychological murk of any relationship environment.

Social support has been proven to have beneficial health effects. A study on the effects of love on health published in the scientific journal, *The Annals of Internal Medicine*, found that emotional support dramatically improved survival after a heart attack. Patients who lacked love and care were more likely to die within six months than patients who experienced love and care in their lives. According to the study's author, Lisa F. Berkman, an epidemiologist at Yale University School of Medicine, "There's enough evidence now to say that lack of social support is a risk factor to the heart, similar to high blood pressure, high cholesterol and lack of exercise."

Freeze-Framing promotes self-maturity through managing mental and emotional energy expenditures in day-to-day relationship and family interactions. Your capacity to do this increases as you *remember* to apply the technique. But if not approached sincerely, you'll frequently forget to practice, especially when you need it.

Sincerity — The Key Factor in Cleaning Up Your Inner Ecology

Sincerity is the amount of heart you focus into a mind intention. For example, when people attempt to forgive others and release the old baggage and resentments, a few days later the same old tired thoughts and feelings often pop up again. This is due to a lack of *continuity* of sincere effort to release and let go of non-efficient thought patterns from the past. Freeze-Framing helps you remember to be sincere in your approach to anything — people, places or issues. Sincerity just means a deeper heart commitment to the task. As I said earlier, heart commitment provides more sustaining power to complete your intention. It assists cleaning out old mental and emotional debris, rewarding you with self-security and esteem. The result is: You feel much better and people around you sense that! As your inner quality improves, the quality of your environment improves. Cleaning up one's inner environment is the most supportive gift people can offer to the outer environment.

Our current scientific research is addressing the possibility that living in the after-effect of stale thoughts and emotions may be far more damaging to people's health than second-hand smoke, hair spray or food additives. You can clean up the air, save the trees and read every dietary label, but until inner mental and emotional rubbish is recycled, there won't be any hope for solving our major problems in social consciousness or achieving "wholeness" health. As you learn to manage your inner ecology, you create a new hormonal balance that generates better health and especially inner peace. That's a direct approach to balancing individual and global stress deficits.

Some people can understand and remember things quickly at the mind level, then forget to apply what they know at the heart level. I realize you may be tired of me bringing up the reminder to *practice*, because you probably feel you've grasped it and don't need to hear it again.Repetition usually addresses key factors that people forget when it comes to hands-on application. So my repetition is not because I've run out of new things to say. It's because of care, wanting you to gain results from the technique. For the good of us all, I'll discipline myself and try not to mention practicing again, as long as you'll remember to practice and watch the results unfold.

Time Shift / Paradigm Shift

The energy you save when you stop and learn to make more effective decisions creates a time shift or "paradigm shift." In this decade of rapid change, there is much discussion in business and government of the need for a global paradigm shift. A paradigm shift is a fundamental change in perspective. It's going from the mind level to the heart intuitive level. Not only does your perspective change, but so does the time it takes to achieve an effective outcome. You save time as perspective broadens (as we discussed in Chapter Three). A fun way to look at a time shift is to recall: 1) what happens when you negatively identify with a situation, 2) the problems that creates, and 3) how long it takes to pick up the pieces. An ineffective decision seals you into standard linear time and creates an energy payload deficit of stress and time loss.

Freeze-Framing allows you a porthole through which to make an energy-saving time shift and paradigm shift. When dealing with situations, stop and listen more deeply from the heart, then discover how to make attitude adjustments in the moment — meaning before-the-fact rather than after-the-fact. Attitude adjustments in the moment tame and manage impulsive reactions to people, places and issues. It's no different than saying to children, "Stop, look and listen before you cross the street." If you really learn to pause, you can weigh out issues consciously rather than reactively. Then, as you tell children, you can look both ways (head and heart) before moving into an action with its resulting consequences. Unweighed reactions to life's situations are a form of sleepwalking. It doesn't have to be that way if people sincerely don't want it to be. However, efforts without sincerity are like attempting to quench your thirst with water that turns to sand as it passes your lips.

People are well aware that they can get into a mess, but not necessarily aware that they can decrease their vulnerability to stresses and messes. Well, they can. We're making much progress in laboratory research proving that people can self-empower at the scientific level, and developing techniques that facilitate access to one's own spirit within. When you deprive your spirit, mental and emotional aging accelerates, diminishing the fun and textures of experience. Multitudes live for survival and fake their fun. The lack of fun strangles nourishment to your mental, emotional and physical natures. Learning to follow your heart, and balancing the mind's request, replenishes you in a wholeness way, reactivating fun and flexibility, and creating a more active spirit. Research is showing that the development of coherence within your inner nature nourishes your whole system right down to the biological cellular level. I'll explain the scientific implications more in another book, *Quantum Intelligence**.

Quantum Intelligence: The Physics of Humanity, by Doc Lew Childre. Available 1996, Planetary Publications.

The Need For Hope

For millions of people, day-to-day existence is an endless treadmill going nowhere fast. For some it's like being lost at sea battling high waves. Here's an analogy:

Adrift in the ocean, you and your partner paddle your life raft for days in search of land. Finally you're both so worn out neither of you can lift the oars anymore. All hope of finding land is lost and you give up. You're lying on the bottom of the boat waiting to die. You look up and see a patch of land. Hope! This one drop of hope renews your strength and vitality to vigorously paddle to reach the land, whereas one minute before you were exhausted and dying.

Hopeful thoughts, emotions and attitudes act to refurbish energy levels. Hopeless thoughts and attitudes sap energy and short circuit your capacity to be creative, whether in the workplace or anyplace. People comment, "How can you not have hopeless attitudes if life seems so hopeless?" Many are discovering that following their hearts starts to restore hope in their mental-emotional system. This, in turn, can affect the physical system as a healing tonic and preventive maintenance against many illnesses.

Increasingly, scientific research is confirming the crucial role of positive emotions and hope in relieving stress and improving health. Yale epidemiologist, Lisa Berkman, Ph.D., also found that positive emotional support alters levels of brain chemicals norepinephrine and cortisol (often called the stress hormone). Although the exact role of those chemicals on the heart is still being investigated, they are believed to affect blood pressure and the heart's response to stress. Leading investigator,

Jeffrey S. Levin, Ph.D., associate professor of family and community medicine at Eastern Virginia Medical School, compiled over two hundred and fifty published, empirical studies that show statistical relationships between positive attitude, spirituality and various positive health outcomes. According to Levin, while social support is key, a sense of hope and a capacity for forgiveness help people cope more effectively with stress.

Just before this book was due at the printers, a news bulletin announced the results of a major medical study at Duke University based on a follow-up of 1,719 people who had been diagnosed with heart disease. The statistics revealed that "a healthy outlook helps heal the heart" while "pessimism can be a killer." The study "identified optimism as a powerful predictor of who will live and who will die after the diagnosis of heart disease." According to heart specialist Daniel Mark, M.D.,

"When people give up and feel they are not going to make it, it's usually a self-fulfilling prophecy.... The mind is a tremendous tool or weapon, depending on your point of view."

Hope for peace and more quality in life is within one's own heart, but without learning to listen to your heart this hope cannot be realized in its completeness. My intention is to provide tools that help people listen to their hearts and actualize hope in practical day-to-day life — in business, social, and personal interactions.

Often people's lack of peace and frustration comes from being in their heart consciousness one day, then in their mind consciousness the next day concerning the same issue. Frequently what they think is their mind is their heart and what they think is their heart is their mind.

It's hard to know the difference until you stop at each issue to take a deeper look. Freeze-Framing is a simple technology for that in-depth scan, providing a more personal connection with your real feelings rather than your reactive responses.

FREEZE-FRAME is not a magic wand, it's just an opportunity — a chance to listen to your heart in situations. Nevertheless, it's you who has to make the choice to follow your heart. The magic in life comes when you have the power to recognize a heart choice and act on it. As I've said, people suffer from recurring stressor patterns even while their hearts are telling them to make changes. It's the unmanaged mind that represses the heart's promptings, while blaming other people and issues for your continuous misery or lack of peace. As this process continues, it creates hopelessness and despair in different areas of your life.

You can fool others and pretend happiness on the outside, yet on the inside you really know if you feel good and are having a quality life — or not. If you FREEZE-FRAME and listen to your heart more, you change those mind-initiated stressor patterns into self-security and quality within your existing environmental conditions. As you make efforts, yet fall back some, don't beat yourself. Self-beating destroys hope more rapidly than other people can with their comments and attitudes. Self-beating seems justified at the mind level, yet your heart knows that self-judgment only multiplies stress and unhappiness. You can stop that through Freeze-Framing, but don't expect total relief from a single effort.

There is hope to change self-defeating patterns. That hope is within you. As you make attempts toward *inter-*

nal change, you take more of the distortion out of your *external* relationships. Being true to your heart feelings, you escape much of the stress that comes from the mind running the show. A humor in life is that people fear mind control, yet they're under siege by *their own* mind's control without the partnership of their heart feelings. It's through heart listening that you learn to become your real Self and be free. The heart directs the mind to help create and decorate that achievement.

The new man and new woman will be the ones who have learned to follow their hearts and bring their minds into management. As psychology evolves, humanity will realize that real freedom is creating a lasting joint adventure and partnership between the heart and the head. Freeze-Framing is a facilitator to help engineer that freedom and create the real paradigm shift — the individual shift — first.

I sincerely hope you have fun and effective results with FREEZE-FRAME. The FREEZE-FRAME process is within you by nature. This system is only a facilitator to help you recall and use the power of your own heart discrimination. The strength and hope you are looking for is also within you; it just needs to be dusted off and oiled on occasion. People get so involved in taking care of the externals in life, they forget to take care of their own mental and emotional self which is where your real peace, quality and fun is registered. So "taking care of self" (inner self) is productive — and it's cost-effective. I'm wholeheartedly wanting to say, "Just practice Freeze-Framing and the results will find you."

The Doc

Appendix

The HeartMath System

At the Institute of HeartMath, we provide trainings, consultations, workbooks, and support materials on FREEZE-FRAME and other HeartMath tools. FREEZE-FRAME is one of the key tools that make up the complete HeartMath system. The mission of the Institute is essentially to develop simple, applicable and effective techniques for tapping into your own reservoir of empowerment. This way you become your own stress buster and a more conscious captain of your own ship.

Our stated mission is to use the combination of science, philosophy and psychology to help put the heart back into the people business. Philosophy and psychology can come up short in practical effectiveness because of the lack of a scientific bottom-line or people who have actualized the proof of a process. The staff at the Institute committed themselves to years of research and application in proving the effectiveness of the HeartMath system before marketing it.

The purpose of the HeartMath system is to supply self-initiated methods to de-stress the human psychological system. My book, *Self-Empowerment,* goes into more of these tools and the overall concept of what the HeartMath system is about. It's simply written, but with the rapid increase of stress on the planet, simple fast action stress relief will soon be in vogue.

FREEZE-FRAME is just one technique HeartMath provides, but a key component because of the amount of stress it can release and the energy it can add to your day. The other key elements in the total HeartMath system are also being proven effective in laboratory research. These tools are just starting to be marketed through books and seminars that serve a wide range of people — from educators to the military, businesses, teenagers, relationships, government, etc. People inform us they need and want something that is especially simple and works **now!**

This appendix contains more stories from adults and children who experienced dramatic changes in their quality of life, using FREEZE-FRAME. These added commentaries give a broader feel of people's personal experiences. We receive many stories from people who enthusiastically share how much FREEZE-FRAME has helped them. The staff at the Institute of HeartMath uses Freeze-Framing and other HeartMath tools not only to manage and prevent stress, but to enhance creativity and intuitive insight on the job and at home.

Dealing with the Shock of the LA Earthquake

Here's another story of living through the massive Los Angeles earthquake of 1994, and how FREEZE-FRAME helped.

"The thing that is helpful about Freeze-Framing to me is the feeling that I don't have to be boxed in feeling like I am a total victim of what is happening around me. It brings 'hope' that, with practice, I will gain mastery over my mental and emotional nature instead of it running me. It's the recognition that by my own choice, I do have some power and say in the situation to determine my own reaction and the amount of energy I leak over it. I have found growth in the speed with which I was able to recover from the whole earthquake/aftershocks situation in L.A. In [the San Fernando Valley earthquake of] 1971, it was months before I recovered, and now using this technique, it was more like hours (for the big one) and minutes and seconds for the small ones.

"I got a new perspective of understanding that Life loves me as much as anyone else, and isn't 'out to get me' — more of an objectivity about what was happening. I also gained a wider perspective of how much worse it could have been and wasn't. FREEZE-FRAME for me is the hope of a wider, broader perspective, whether I see it right in that moment or not. But it's that wider perspective and understanding that helps me feel that everything really is O.K."
L.D., legal secretary, Los Angeles, CA

Taking Care of the Care-Givers

A staff of mental health counselors received a

HeartMath training at an Army post. Several months later, an IHM employee talked to their chief of staff. He said that all the counselors began using FREEZE-FRAME with their clients and were helping their clients gain clarity with this tool. Here's his comment:

> "After a while, we began using it in our staff meetings too, and found the tool particularly helpful. The counselors saw the importance of reminding each other of the FREEZE-FRAME tool — always remembering that it is an option they have available at any moment. It has helped them, as caregivers, help each other take better care of themselves. In my experience, it's quite common for caregivers to share their skills with clients, but often forget to do what they need to take care of themselves. The simplicity of FREEZE-FRAME is excellent for that."
> D.W., Atlanta, GA

Resolving Old Family Conflicts

This story was conveyed by a woman who attended a HeartMath training at an Air Force Base.

> "I had just returned from a family visit over Christmas. Upon arriving, I was faced with the same old things that have always caused me to dread these family gatherings. People complaining, judgments being made, and nobody getting along. I remembered FREEZE-FRAME and went right into the steps. I was able to stay balanced and remember how much I loved them. That visit proved to me that FREEZE-FRAME works and helped me have the best Christmas I can ever remember."
> L.K. Anchorage, AK

How Children Use FREEZE-FRAME

I thought you would especially enjoy some stories from children. Now there's no excuse — simple enough for a child to use, but powerful enough to take on corporations.

"Today in this seminar I really liked the idea of FREEZE-FRAME. I tried it during my history class when this boy was acting really dumb. I felt like hitting him, and then I remembered, and I paused every thought I had and started thinking only about my family and how I loved them and they loved me. I calmed down and smiled. Hitting him just wasn't important. I'm sure this Institute helped the teachers today and will help many more people during the next seminars."
Tony, 13

"Once I was getting really mad because I was stressed out. I couldn't get this one little answer in math on this really hard paper. Then the teacher said, 'Recess time,' and I still wasn't done. I got so upset that I told myself FREEZE-FRAME. Then I wrote down the right answer. Another time I was running in my bare feet to the kitchen to get a snack and I stubbed my toe on the bumpy concrete. I went, 'Ow, Ow' and my toe was bleeding. It had hurt so bad I was almost crying. So I sat down on one of the stairs and did my FREEZE-FRAME. I sent heart to my toe and it helped a lot. FREEZE-FRAME made me feel happy instead of sad."
Elysia, 7

How Parents Use FREEZE-FRAME

"FREEZE-FRAME has been the single most helpful, satisfying parenting tool I have ever used. It shifts life in the direction I most want — towards connection, understanding and fun with minimal conflict and without smothering the child or compromising myself.

"When a parent and child fly on a commercial airline, they tell you that in an emergency the parent should put her own oxygen mask on first, then help the child put on his. As a parent, this goes against the grain of instinct that tells you to put the child's safety first. But there's wisdom in these rules: As a parent you aren't much use to the child if you can't breathe. So, the first responsibility for a parent would be to attend to your own balance in order to be of maximum service to your child.

"When I first began using FREEZE-FRAME with my daughter, I was more concerned with her learning and applying the tool. When she would get upset, angry, sad or frustrated, I would ask her to FREEZE-FRAME. Sometimes she could, sometimes she couldn't. Then I realized I had to shift my priorities to first establishing my own balance — making sure I was calm, listening deeply, not reacting or 'needing to fix her.' The effect on her has been amazing. I have learned that no matter how upset she is, how suddenly a situation erupts, or how compelling it may feel to 'fix' her attitude, I need to take a moment to check in with myself first, and FREEZE-FRAME. This calms any impatience, judgment, over-concern, or frustration. It helps me sincerely listen with compassion and care and see what's ultimately best for her. My communication is much more effective and she gets the message faster.

"Freeze-Framing can greatly facilitate the parenting process, so that the dozens of messages you pass on to the kids everyday, like the little fine-tune pointers, admonitions and encouragements, are empowered and their understanding accelerated by coming more directly from the heart. The first time you try this, especially if it's at a trying time, you may have to remind yourself to FREEZE-FRAME ten times in a five minute period. But that's OK, it gets easier, more automatic and natural. The more consistently I am in my heart and use FREEZE-FRAME to manage the times I'm not, the easier her life is and the better her relationships are, especially with me."
S.C., publicist, Santa Cruz, CA

And How Was Your Day?

A staff person at the Institute had a very unusual experience recently while running errands with a tight time deadline. Here is her story.

"While sitting in my car waiting for a parking space to open up, I was run down by a self-starting, 'possessed' Ford Bronco. This car literally ignited all by itself and drove right into the rear side of my car. That's right, there were no passengers astride that Bronco. But I was trapped inside my car. The truck from hell was slammed up against my door. Then as I was sitting there, its battery exploded spitting acid everywhere. I started to feel the adrenaline surge inside my body — and the reality that my beautiful red sports car was now smashed and there was nothing I could do about it. I could feel my body start to tremble and my mind raced with thoughts of panic.

"Then it struck me — a perfect time to FREEZE-FRAME! Instantly the energy inside began to calm down and I realized I had two choices: one was to freak out and the other was to play this out real cool. I chose the cool modality. A few seconds passed and a man came to my rescue. He guided me to turn my wheels to the left and move forward an inch, then back three inches, stating that this would free my car from the jaws of the white Bronco. Instead this only aggravated the situation. I managed to get myself out of my car to assess the damage. The sight of my car brought back the flood of adrenaline. 'FREEZE-FRAME!' said my inner voice. I took a deep breath, closed my eyes and just stood there, consciously bringing the energy to my heart. Comforting thoughts and feelings that 'Everything is going be all right, this really is no big deal, nothing to stay upset about,' warmed my system. I felt a large portion of anxiety leave my body. I was ready to take action. I wrote down the license plate number, the make of the car and set out to call the police. I wondered if the owner was going to return soon and would he or she be cooperative. I was even beginning to have fun with the whole bizarre situation. Soon the owner of the car walked up. At first she was a little upset but it didn't take long for her to realize that this situation was too weird to get really bummed out about. She even commented that she was grateful that I had been such a good sport. The policeman arrived shortly thereafter and was helpful and courteous. Freeze-Framing the circumstances allowed me to make the best of the situation and let go of the hustle and bustle day I'd previously planned."

M.S., *receptionist, IHM*

What a Day!

"I was scheduled to give a featured keynote presentation to educators and professors from over 40 countries at a large international conference in Stockholm, Sweden. Naturally, I was very excited about this event and put in a lot of preparation time. About an hour before the presentation, I discovered that I had left all my preparation notes at my contact's home which would be impossible to retrieve in such a short time. I immediately began to feel nervous and panicky. All the great ideas I had were now unavailable. To make matters worse, the video tape that I brought from America would not work on the video equipment at this conference.

"'Wow!' I said to myself. 'This is getting crazy. I came all the way from America to give a keynote presentation only to forget my notes and the video tape won't even work. What am I going to do? I can't possibly deliver a presentation of good quality off the top of my head without any support documentation.' Sweat beads formed around my forehead. My mind began racing with what I could say or what backup plans I might put into place. Because my mind was moving so fast and my emotions bursting with nervousness, I couldn't really get a clear or cohesive picture of what I might do — only scattered images. 'I've got to hurry,' I kept saying to myself. 'Time is of the essence.'

"I raced to the bathroom. As I approached the entrance, I took a giant 'banana peel' slip on the just washed linoleum floor. I landed almost horizontally, putting most of my weight on my left hip. A sharp pain throbbed from the hip area. My immediate thoughts were that I had broken my hip, so strong was the pain. I managed to get up and drag myself over to a nearby table. The hip seemed to be working but it was badly bruised.

"I had 30 minutes to get my act together and it wasn't looking very good. My emotional and mental states could not have been in worse condition, not to mention my body aches. Full panic set in. I had to FREEZE-FRAME, there was no other option right now. Getting myself together became a higher priority than organizing a presentation. I closed my eyes and took a series of deep breaths. 'Just be quiet for a few moments,' I said to myself. 'Relax as best as you can. Try to hear the advice of the heart as the mind is too scattered and fast to be coherent.' I listened to the heart and chilled my mind for several minutes. Out of the quiet came a surprising calm and some clarity about which way to proceed. I realized that I knew what I needed to say pretty well after all. And I liked people, period. That could be fun. 'Give yourself some slack. You will do all right. Be sincere with the attendees about what happened. They will understand.'

"As it turned out, the presentation went very well. People responded to my sincerity and to the value of the information shared. It went without a hitch. FREEZE-FRAME rescued me. It demonstrated that there is a reservoir of strength and clarity within my heart that can be tapped instantly if I just re-

member. Stepping back from those panic-ridden moments for just a few minutes brought a high return during that day — one I will never forget."
J.G., *Author, The Ultimate Kid*

A Flight Attendant Handles a Near-Disaster

"It was June 1993. I had turned in my resignation to the airline which employed me and was on my next to last flight as a flight attendant. We were traveling to Tokyo, I was Chief Purser on our 747-400, packed with over 300 people. Six hours into the flight, I received a call from the cockpit. The captain said he needed to talk to me for a few minutes. He said we had lost engine #4 and were having problems with engine #3. There was a possibility that we would have to prepare the cabin for a ditching in the ocean. I needed to tell the crew, but he did not plan to tell the passengers (who were all asleep) until he was certain whether or not #3 would remain working.

"This was definitely a time for FREEZE-FRAME! I needed to collect myself so I could deliver the news to the in-flight crew, handle their response and plan the evacuation. I had to prepare myself for the reaction of the passengers. I knew from practice, FREEZE-FRAME would slow me down, give me a wider perspective on the situation and allow me to deal with the problem more efficiently. I also wanted to calm down my inner feelings. I was close to leaving the airlines and I could really have gone wild with my thoughts of this being my LAST flight (no pun intended). I was going to a new job and was really looking forward to my new life. And here I was, about to prepare for landing in the ocean!

"The FREEZE-FRAME helped me slow myself down, so I felt balanced enough to handle the situation calmly and effectively. As it turned out, they were able to restart engine #3. The captain told the passengers we were having engine trouble and would have to land in Alaska and spend the night to get the engine fixed. The passengers never knew about the possible ditching, but were very upset about spending the night in Alaska. I was glad I had done my FREEZE-FRAME because it helped me deal with their anger so I didn't react and get caught up in their reactions. Some of them were not about to be talked out of their anger, so all I could do was send some compassion their way. There wasn't any way I could change the situation but it felt good to remain at peace inside myself. Of course, from my perspective, I was so grateful we didn't have to take that dip in the Pacific."
T.H., Redondo Beach, CA.

About the Institute of HeartMath Research

The Institute of HeartMath is a nonprofit educational and research corporation founded by Doc Lew Childre, a leading researcher in human development, and noted author and composer. IHM's mission is to *put the heart back in the people business.* For centuries, the word *heart* has been associated with the source of life, courage, wisdom, and intuition, as well as the feelings of love, care, and appreciation. IHM has pioneered new biomedical research showing the relationship between feelings, the heart, mental/emotional balance, cardiovascular function, and hormonal and immune system health. Under the direction of Doc Lew Childre, IHM's Research Division is exploring the central role the heart's electrical system plays in health and well-being. This research has profound implications in helping you become more effective and fulfilled in all that you do.

The Institute's Physics of Humanity Council and Scientific Advisory Board are composed of esteemed scientists in the fields of cardiology, neurology, immunology, quantum physics, and psychology, who provide invaluable insights and expertise on IHM research projects. These studies involve hypertensive and cardiac patients, individuals with hormonal imbalances, individuals living with HIV or AIDS, as well as joint venture studies in partnership with major corporations researching how human performance and effectiveness can be greatly improved as people learn the tools of the HeartMath system.

IHM's research has been presented at a number of national and international conferences, including the Seventh International Montreux Congress on Stress, the Armed Forces Communication & Electronics Association (AFCEA) 1994 Europe Symposium, and the annual meetings of the American Psychosomatic Society and the Academy of Psychosomatic Medicine. Published research studies and scientific papers in press include the following:

Published Research Studies

G. Rein, R. McCraty. Long Term Effects of Compassion on Salivary IgA. *Psychosomatic Medicine*, 56: 2, 171-72, abst, 1994.

G. Rein, R. McCraty. Structural Changes in Water and DNA Associated with New Physiologically Measurable States. *Journal of Scientific Exploration*, 8:3, 438-39, 1994.

R. McCraty, D.L. Childre. Efficient Communication with Anyone, Anywhere, Any Time — Freeze-Frame: A One-Minute, Scientifically Validated Stress Reduction Technique. 1994 Proceedings: *Armed Forces Communication and Electronics Assoc.*, Budapest, Hungary.

R. McCraty, M. Atkinson, W.A. Tiller. New Electrophysiological Correlates Associated With Intentional Heart Focus. *Subtle Energies*, 4:2, 251-69, 1995.

Scientific Papers in Press

D. Rozman, R. Whitaker, T. Beckman, and D. Jones. Initial Use of a New Intervention Program for Significantly Reducing Psychological Symptomatology in HIV-Seropositive Individuals. *Psychosomatics*, Long Abstract In Press, 1995.

R. McCraty, M. Atkinson, W. A. Tiller, and G. Rein. Autonomic Assessment of Emotional States Using Power Spectral Analysis of Heart Rate Variability. *Journal of Biofeedback and Self Regulation*, In Press, 1995.

R. McCraty, M. Atkinson, W. A. Tiller, G. Rein, and A. Watkins. The Effects of Emotions on Short Term Power Spectrum Analysis of Heart Rate Variability. *Psychosomatic Medicine*, Long Asbstract In Press, 1995.

G. Rein, R. Mc Craty, M. Atkinson. The Physiological and Psychological Effects of Compassion and Anger. *Journal of Advancement in Medicine*, In Press, 1995.

Funding

IHM research is supported by private donations, as well as foundations and corporations. IHM is a 501 (c) (3) nonprofit corporation; donations are tax-deductible. Donations of any size are gratefully received to accelerate these research efforts.

About Our Clients

The Institute provides thousands of hours of training programs each year to organizations in both the public and private sectors. Our clients include Fortune 100 companies, governmental agencies, military bases, human service, educational, and religious institutions. Here is a partial list of organizations whose staff have attended IHM programs:

Business & Industry

Adobe Systems
Advanced Cardiovascular
  Systems
Apple Computer
Arthur Andersen
AT&T
Cadence Systems
Dresser Industries
Herman Miller, Inc.
Hitachi
Instromedix
Levi Strauss & Co.
Lockheed

Mainstream Access Corp.
Mechanics Bank
Motorola
National Semiconductor
Northern Telecom
Packard Bell
Seagate Technology
SmithKline Beecham
Sun Microsystems
Teleservices Resources
Transamerica
U.S. Chamber of Commerce
Young Presidents Organization

Government, Education & Community

1994 School of Addictions (Alaska)
Alaska Staff Development Network
American Holistic Nurses Assn.
California Dept. of Mental Health
California Youth Authority
California Teacher's Association
Center for International Dialogue
Central California Women's Facility
Dade County Public Schools
DeKalb School District

Government, Education & Community (continued)

Florida Department of Health & Rehabilitation
Fulton County Detention Center
LA County Gang Risk Intervention
LA County Office of Education
Los Angeles City Attorney's Office
Mexican-American Community Service Association
Migrant Education — Los Angeles, Salinas, San Jose
Pepperdine University
Post-Disaster Crisis Counselors, Miami
Sacramento Court and Community Schools
San Francisco Unified School District
San Mateo County Office of Education
Santa Clara County Office of Education
U.S. Air Force — Andrews, Elmendorf, Falcon, McClellan, Travis
U.S. Army — AMEDD Center and School, Forts Irwin, Hood, Polk,
    Richardson, Rucker, Sam Houston
U.S. Marine Corps — Barstow Logistics, Camp Pendleton
U.S. Navy — Naval Postgraduate School, Alameda, Treasure Island,
    Pearl Harbor
University of Colorado
University of San Diego

FREEZE-FRAME® PRODUCTS & PROGRAMS

FREEZE-FRAME WORKSHOPS

FREEZE-FRAME® workshops provide hands-on instruction and practical applications of the FREEZE-FRAME technique. These powerful and practical half-day programs are available on-site for corporations, governmental agencies and public institutions through certified HeartMath® trainers and at IHM's research facility. Call for more information.

FREEZE-FRAME RESEARCH/TRAINING VIDEO

This powerful training video features an in-depth presentation of the leading-edge scientific research behind FREEZE-FRAME along with step-by-step instruction and personal interviews from professionals illustrating the impact and diverse applications of this innovative self-management technique. Used alone or as part of meetings, special programs or training sessions, this high-quality tool is an excellent resource for trainers, consultants and organizations in need of stress management, team building, improved customer service, organizational development, enhanced communication skills and project planning. *$595.00 plus shipping and handling ($40.00 preview fee), lease/purchase agreements available*

FREEZE-FRAME WORKSHEETS

A convenient, easy-to-use form for written FREEZE-FRAME exercises. Encourages faster development of FREEZE-FRAME skill. *$6.95 (pad of 50 work sheets)*

TRAINING PROGRAMS, RETREATS AND CONSULTING SERVICES

The FREEZE-FRAME seminar is one module of the HeartMath®
training programs conducted by IHM for businesses, organizations,
agencies and individuals. Other HeartMath programs are also available in communication skills, team empowerment, project planning, sales, care vs. overcare, and other customized modules.

Personal and corporate retreats are held at the Institute's research facility in the Santa Cruz Mountains of central California.
Nestled among redwood forests just 45 minutes from the San Jose
Airport, Institute programs offer rejuvenating, relaxing opportunities to learn the HeartMath tools for personal efficiency, fulfillment and greater effectiveness. Programs include:

♦ Inner Quality Management®
♦ Women's Empowerment
♦ The Empowered Relationship™
♦ Heart Empowerment®
♦ The Empowered Parent
♦ Men's Empowerment

♦ Managing Change,
  Enhancing Quality
♦ Heart of Health Care™
♦ Heart of Service™
♦ Heart Smarts®

Consulting services are also available for individuals and businesses through certified HeartMath trainers.

For complete information on IHM training programs, products, consulting services, and customized modules, call, write or
fax:

INSTITUTE OF HEARTMATH
14700 West Park Avenue
Boulder Creek, California 95006
(408) 338-8700 fax (408) 338-9861
Internet: hrtmath@netcom.com

BOOKS AND MUSIC FROM PLANETARY PUBLICATIONS

SELF EMPOWERMENT: The Heart Approach to Stress Management
By Doc Lew Childre

Presents overall concept of HeartMath along with common sense strategies and practical solutions for increasing quality both personally and professionally in the high stress '90s. *$13.95*

"The message is a strong one and the methodology can be understood by many. The potential release of positive energy is formidable."
J. TRACY O'ROURKE, CHAIRMAN AND CEO, VARIAN ASSOCIATES, INC.

THE HOW TO BOOK OF TEEN SELF DISCOVERY
By Doc Lew Childre

Offers a common ground for improved communication, building a bridge for adult/teen bonding. Written in a language that both teens and adults can relate to, *Teen Self Discovery* explores practical tools that develop true self-security leading to a more balanced, mature approach to life for young adults. *$9.95*

"Groundbreaking...Powerful...Fun"
COLLEGE PREVIEW: A GUIDE FOR COLLEGE & CAREER BOUND STUDENTS

THE HIDDEN POWER OF THE HEART
By Sara Paddison

Delivers a brilliant blend of modern science and personal growth techniques in a warm, real life story that is entertaining, informational and expansive. This book is a life changing experience that speaks to the reader like a best friend. *$11.95*

"Sara Paddison's book will revitalize the truth whereby one can not only consult one's heart but can actually listen to what it says. This book should be required reading."
DR. VERNON H. MARK, DIRECTOR EMERITUS, BOSTON CITY HOSPITAL

HEART ZONES
By Doc Lew Childre

Based on advanced research into human performance, *Heart Zones* is an intelligent blending of creativity and science. This four song musical composition designed to boost vitality and facilitate mental and emotional balance is the first music of its kind—'Designer Music'—to reach the Billboard Charts where it remained for 50 consecutive weeks.
Cassette $9.95, CD $15.95

> *"Like a psychological cup of coffee without the side effects."*
> USA TODAY

NEW!

SPEED OF BALANCE
A Musical Adventure for Emotional & Mental Regeneration
By Doc Lew Childre

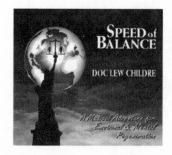

Doc Lew Childre's follow-up to his landmark release *Heart Zones*. *Speed of Balance* features eight new songs that have been arranged to create a cascading effect that leaves the listener with more energy and feeling ready to move on with life. Combining Doc's unique blend of creativity and science, this music helps to balance the emotional and mental natures, enhancing creativity and improving clear decision making. *Speed of Balance* represents the next step in music scientifically designed to care as well as entertain.
Cassette $9.95, CD $15.95

NEW IN SPRING 1995

A PARENTING MANUAL
How To Prevent & Close Communication Gaps at Any Age Through Common Sense & Intuitive Understanding
By Doc Lew Childre

Following the success of his highly acclaimed *How To Book of Teen Self Discovery,* Doc's *Parenting Manual* addresses raising children in the fast-paced '90s — and beyond the year 2000. Doc zeroes in on the stress and lack of hope many children feel, reflected in the chilling statistics on youth violence, crime and suicide. He targets critical developmental stages, offering proven tools for helping children maintain mental and emotional balance. *A Parenting Manual* shows adults *how* to perceive through the eyes of today's children, and cross the barriers that create communication breakdown. It provides tools for parents and youngsters to manage and prevent unbalanced attitudes that cause family disruption and separation. *A Parenting Manual* helps parents develop the *intuitive heart relationship* — the glue that sustains family bonding. $14.95

NEW FOR FALL 1995

CUT-THRU™
Insecurity and Energy Drain
A Scientifically Proven Insight on How To Care
Without Becoming A Victim
By Doc Lew Childre

Millions experience worry, anxiety, or insecurity regarding people and issues they care about. "Unmanaged" care often turns into "overcare" which devitalizes the mental, emotional and physical system, resulting in burnout and accelerated aging. *Cut-Thru* provides a powerful solution—a scientifically proven insight on how to draw the line between care and "overcare" so you stop being a victim of your own doing. Doc presents a simple, new technology that can turn emotional and mental drains and deficits into assets. The *Cut-Thru* technique facilitates fast relief from fear, anxiety, insecurity, and self-beating. Learning to prevent overcare rewards you with mental and emotional empowerment and freedom. It unleashes free energy to increase your quality of life and health. It's simple reading. *$9.95*

ORDERING INFORMATION

   To order books, videos, tapes and compact discs, please send check, money order or credit card information to:

Planetary Publications
P.O. Box 66 • Boulder Creek, California, 95006
800-372-3100/408-338-2161/Fax 408-338-9861

♦ Please include shipping and handling cost:
   $4.50 for first item,
   $1.00 each additional item.
♦ Foreign Orders:
   Please call for accurate shipping rates.
♦ California residents include 7.25% sales tax.
♦ Santa Cruz County residents include 8.25% sales tax.
♦ Visa, Mastercard, Discover Card, and American Express accepted. Please include expiration date, card number, full name on card, and signature.
♦ For convenience, place your order using our toll-free number — 800-372-3100, 24 hours a day, 7 days a week or fax us at 408-338-9861.

NOTES

You've read the Book...Now, own the Video!

The inspiring and informative FREEZE-FRAME® Video is your next step in personal and professional effectiveness. You'll watch this powerful video over and over again, gaining insights that simplify the complexities of life.

The FREEZE-FRAME Video presents the breakthrough technology you just read about in a powerfully motivating 20-minute program. Vivid computer graphics blend with fascinating segments of the science behind FREEZE-FRAME featuring researchers and experts, taking you on a journey to new levels of potential for health and effectiveness.

The FREEZE-FRAME Video is invaluable for organizations, teams, professionals and learning groups. An important addition to your video library that takes you into a new world of clarity, quality, and intuitive insight.

Cost: $595.00

Our friendly representatives will be delighted to answer questions or share stories about how people and organizations are using FREEZE-FRAME.

For more information

phone: 1-800-372-3100

or fax: **1-408-338-9861**

or mail this card to:
Planetary Publications

Name: _____
Organization: _____
Title: _____
Address: _____
City, State,Zip: _____
Phone/FAX : (____) _____

NO POSTAGE
NECESSARY IF
MAILED IN THE
UNITED STATES

BUSINESS REPLY MAIL

FIRST CLASS   PERMIT NO. 50   BOULDER CREEK, CA 95006

POSTAGE WILL BE PAID BY ADDRESSEE

Planetary Publications

P.O. Box 66 Dept. FFBV
Boulder Creek, CA 95006